Ethics and Economics

The Canadian Issues Series

James Lorimer & Company has developed this series of original paperbacks to offer informed, up-to-date, critical introductions to key issues facing Canada and Canadians. Books are written specifically for the series by authors commissioned by the publisher on the basis of their expertise in a subject area and their ability to write for a general audience.

The 4″ x 7″ paperback format and cover design for the series offer attractive books at the lowest possible price. Special library hard-bound editions are also available. New titles are added to the series every spring and fall: watch for them in your local bookstore.

University and community college lecturers interested in forthcoming titles in the series should contact the Lorimer promotion manager.

Already in print:

The West BY J.F. CONWAY
Oil and Gas BY JAMES LAXER
Women and Work BY PAUL PHILLIPS and ERIN PHILLIPS
The New Canadian Constitution BY DAVID MILNE
Regional Disparities (UPDATED EDITION) BY PAUL PHILLIPS
Out of Work BY CY GONICK
Rising Prices BY H. LUKIN ROBINSON
ndustry in Decline BY RICHARD STARKS

nes Lorimer & Company, Publishers

Ethics and Economics

Canada's Catholic Bishops on the Economic Crisis

GREGORY BAUM
DUNCAN CAMERON

James Lorimer & Company, Publishers
Toronto 1984

ISBN 0-88862-704-1 paper
0-88862-705-X cloth

Cover design: Brant Cowie
Cover illustration: © Barbara D. Cummings 1983

Canadian Cataloguing in Publication Data

Baum, Gregory, 1923-
Ethics and economics

(Canadian issues series)
Bibliography: p. 213

1. Canada — Economic policy - 1971- — Moral and ethical aspects.* 2. Catholic Church — Canada — Political activity. 3. Church and state — Canada. I. Cameron, Duncan, 1944- II. Title. III. Series: Canadian issues series (Toronto, Ont.).

HC115.B38 1984 339.5'0971 C84-098204-6

James Lorimer & Company, Publishers
Egerton Ryerson Memorial Building
35 Britain Street
Toronto, Ontario M5A 1R7

Printed and bound in Canada
6 5 4 3 2 1 84 85 86 87 88 89

Contents

Introduction

The lively public response to the Catholic bishops' 1983 New Year's Statement, "Ethical Reflections on the Economic Crisis," and the ongoing debate involving all sectors of Canadian society that it provoked, prompted us to collaborate in the preparation of this little volume. One of us is a Catholic theologian with a special interest in the Christian quest for social justice: he is the author of the first commentary of this volume, concentrating on the statement's religious and cultural meaning. The other is a political economist with a special interest in alternative proposals to the present economic arrangements: he is the author of the second commentary, focusing on the economic issues raised by the bishops and relating them to the evidence provided by political economy. The volume is introduced by the text of "Ethical Reflections on the Economic Crisis."

Since the 1983 statement has emerged from a social theory that has been worked out by the Canadian bishops over the years, four earlier social statements published by the Canadian bishops are included as appendixes. While these document were distributed in parishes and schools when the were released, they are not easily found in print at this time.

It is hoped that the present volume will promote the ethical debate on the Canadian economy, enabling more people to join in this debate. This book is not written in the first place for academics and experts; but, rather, its purpose is to engage the attention of ordinary Canadians whose well-being depends on the present economic arrangements, including vast numbers of unemployed and ever greater numbers of people whose present employment is insecure. The Catholic bishops envisaged their statement as the basis for workshops to be held in congregations, schools, labour organizations and other social institutions. Only as the Canadians who suffer from the present crisis stand together and demand structural change, will the economic system become more benign and serve the well-being of all.

Gregory Baum
Duncan Cameron

The second principle concerns the special value and dignity of human work in God's plan for Creation.[4] It is through the activity of work that people are able to exercise their creative spirit, realize their human dignity, and share in Creation. By interacting with fellow workers in a common task, men and women have an opportunity to further develop their personalities and sense of self-worth. In so doing, people participate in the development of their society and give meaning to their existence as human beings.[5] Indeed, the importance of human labour is illustrated in the life of Jesus who was himself a worker, "a craftsman like Joseph of Nazareth."[6]

It is from the perspective of these basic gospel principles that we wish to share our reflections on the current economic crisis. Along with most people in Canada today, we realize that our economy is in serious trouble. In our own regions, we have seen the economic realities of plant shutdowns, massive layoffs of workers, wage-restraint programs, and suspension of collective-bargaining rights for public sector workers. At the same time, we have seen the social realities of abandoned one-industry towns, depleting unemployment insurance benefits, cutbacks in health and social services, and lineups at local soup kitchens. And, we have also witnessed, first hand, the results of a troubled economy: personal tragedies, emotional strain, loss of human dignity, family breakdown and even suicide.

Indeed, we recognize that serious economic challenges lie ahead for this country. If our society is going to face up to these challenges, people must meet and work together as a "true community" with vision and courage. In developing strategies for economic recovery, we firmly believe that first priority must be given to the real victims of the current recession—namely, the unemployed, the welfare poor, the working poor, pensioners, Native Peoples, women, young people, small farmers, fishermen, some factory workers and some small business men and women. This option calls for economic policies which realize that the needs of the poor have priority over the wants of the rich; that the rights of workers are more important than the maximization of profits; that the participation of marginalized groups has precedence over the preservation of a system which excludes them.

In response to current economic problems, we suggest that priority be given to the following short-term strategies by both government and business.

First, unemployment rather than inflation should be recognized as the number one problem to be tackled in overcoming the present crisis. The fact that some 1.5 million people are jobless constitutes a serious moral as well as economic crisis in this country. While efforts should continually be made to curb wasteful spending, it is imperative that primary emphasis be placed on combatting unemployment.

Second, an industrial strategy should be developed to create permanent and meaningful jobs for people in local communities. To be effective, such a strategy should be designed at both national and regional levels. It should include emphasis on increased production, creation of new labour-intensive industries for basic needs and measures to ensure job security for workers.

Third, a more balanced and equitable program

should be developed for reducing and stemming the rate of inflation. This requires shifting the burden for wage controls to upper income earners and introducing controls on prices and new forms of taxes on investment income (e.g., dividends, interest).

Fourth, greater emphasis should be given to the goal of social responsibility in the current recession. This means that every effort must be made to curtail cutbacks in social services, maintain adequate health care and social security benefits, and, above all, guarantee special assistance for the unemployed, welfare recipients, the working poor and one-industry towns suffering from plant shutdowns.

Fifth, labour unions should be asked to play a more decisive and responsible role in developing strategies for economic recovery and employment. This requires the restoration of collective-bargaining rights where they have been suspended, collaboration between unions and the unemployed and unorganized workers, and assurances that labour unions will have an effective role in developing economic policies.

Furthermore, all people of good will in local and regional communities throughout the country must be encouraged to coordinate their efforts to develop and implement such strategies. As a step in thi direction, we again call on local Christian commu nities to become actively involved in the six-poi plan of action outlined in the message of t Canadian bishops on "Unemployment: The Hum Costs."[7] [The six-point plan appears at the end this statement; and "Unemployment: The Hur Costs" is included as Appendix 4—ed.]

We recognize that these proposals run counter to some current policies or strategies advanced by both governments and corporations. We are also aware of the limited perspectives and excessive demands of some labour unions. To be certain, the issues are complex; there are no simple or magical solutions. Yet, from the standpoint of the Church's social teachings,[8] we firmly believe that present economic realities reveal a "moral disorder" in our society. As pastors, we have a responsibility to raise some of the fundamental social and ethical issues pertaining to the economic order. In so doing, we expect that there will be considerable discussion and debate within the Christian community itself on these issues. Indeed, we hope that the following reflections will help to explain our concerns and contribute to the current public debate about the economy.

2: The Economic Crisis

The present recession appears to be symptomatic of a much larger structural crisis in the international system of capitalism. Observers point out that profound changes are taking place in the structure of both capital and technology which are bound to have serious social impacts on labour.[9] We are now in an age, for example, where transnational corporations and banks can move capital from one country to another in order to take advantage of cheaper labour conditions, lower taxes and reduced environmental restrictions. We are also in an age of automation and computers, where human work is rapidly being replaced by machines on the assembly line and in administrative centres. In effect, capital has become transnational and technology has become increasingly capital intensive. The consequences are likely to be permanent or structural unemployment and increasing marginalization for a large segment of the population in Canada and other countries.[10] In this context, the increasing concentration of capital and technology in the production of military armaments further intensifies this economic crisis, rather than bringing about recovery.[11]

Indeed, these structural changes largely explain the nature of the current economic recession at home and throughout the world.[12] While there does not appear to be global shortage of capital per se, large-scale banks and corporations continue to wait for a more profitable investment climate. Many companies are also experiencing a temporary shortage of investment funds required for the new technology, due largely to an overextension of production and related factors. In order to restore profit margins needed for new investment, companies are cutting back on production, laying off workers and selling off their inventories. The result has been economic slowdown and soaring unemployment. To stimulate economic growth, governments are being called upon to provide a more favourable climate for private investments. Since capital tends to flow wherever the returns are greatest, reduced labour costs and lower taxes are required if countries are to remain competitive. As a result, most governments are introducing austerity measures, such as wage-restraint programs, cutbacks in social services and other reductions in social spending, in order to attract more private investment. And to enforce such economic policies some countries have introduced repressive mea sures for restraining civil liberties and controlling social unrest.

3: Moral Crisis

The current structural changes in the global economy, in turn, reveal a deepening moral crisis. Through these structural changes, "capital" is reasserted as the dominant organizing principle of economic life. This orientation directly contradicts the ethical principle that labour, not capital, must be given priority in the development of an economy based on justice.[13] There is, in other words, an ethical order in which human labour, the subject of production, takes precedence over capital and technology. This is the *priority of labour* principle. By placing greater importance on the accumulation of profits and machines than on the people who work in a given economy, the value, meaning and dignity of human labour is violated. By creating conditions for permanent unemployment, an increasingly large segment of the population is threatened with the loss of human dignity. In effect, there is a tendency for people to be treated as an impersonal force having little or no significance beyond their economic purpose in the system.[14] As long as technology and capital are not harnessed by society to serve basic human needs, they are likely to become an enemy rather than an ally in the development of peoples.[15]

In addition, the renewed emphasis on the "survival of the fittest" as the supreme law of economics is likely to increase the domination of the weak by the strong, both at home and abroad. The "survival of the fittest" theory has often been used to rationalize the increasing concentration of wealth and power in the hands of a few.[16] The strong survive, the weak are eliminated. Under conditions of "tough competition" in international markets for capital and trade, the poor majority of the world is especially vulnerable. With three-quarters of the world's population, for example, the poor nations of the South are already expected to survive on less than one-fifth of the world's income. Within Canada itself, the top 20 per cent of the population receive 42.5 per cent of total personal income, while the bottom 20 per cent receive 4.1 per cent.[17] These patterns of domination and inequality are likely to further intensify as the "survival of the fittest" doctrine is applied more rigorously to the economic order. While these Darwinian theories partly explain the rules that govern the animal world, they are in our view morally unacceptable as a "rule of life" for the human community.

4: Present Strategies

There is a very real danger that these same structural and moral problems are present in Canada's strategies for economic recovery. As recent economic policy statements reveal, the primary objective is to restore profitability and competitiveness in certain Canadian industries and provide more favourable conditions for private investment in the country.[18] The private sector is to be the "engine" for economic recovery. To achieve these goals, inflation is put forth as the number one problem. The causes of inflation are seen as workers' wages, government spending and low productivity rather than monopoly control of prices. The means for curbing inflation are such austerity measures as the federal 6-and-5 wage-restraint program and cutbacks in social spending (e.g., hospitals, medicare, public services, education and foreign aid), rather than controls on profits and prices.[19] These measures, in turn, have been strengthened by a series of corporate tax reductions and direct investment incentives for such sectors as the petroleum industry. In effect, the survival of capital takes priority over labour in present strategies for economic recovery.

At the same time, working people, the unemployed, young people, and those on fixed incomes are increasingly called upon to make the most sacrifice for economic recovery. For it is these people who suffer most from layoffs, wage restraints, and cutbacks in social services. The recent tax changes, which have the effect of raising taxes for working people and lowering them for the wealthy, add to this burden. And these conditions, in turn, are reinforced by the existence of large-scale unemployment, which tends to generate a climate of social fear and passive acceptance. Moreover, the federal and provincial wage-control programs are inequitable, imposing the same control rate on lower incomes as on upper incomes.[20] If successfully implemented, these programs could also have the effect of transferring income from wages to profits.[21] Yet, there are no clear reasons to believe that working people will ever really benefit from these and other sacrifices they are called to make. For even if companies recover and increase their profit margins, the additional revenues are likely to be reinvested in some labour-saving technology, exported to other countries or spent on market speculation or luxury goods.

5: Alternative Approaches

An alternative approach calls for a reordering of values and priorities in our economic life. What is required first is a basic shift in values: the goal of serving the human needs of all people in our society must take precedence over the maximization of profits and growth, and priority must be given to the dignity of human labour, not machines.[22] From this perspective, economic policies that focus primary attention on inflation and treat soaring unemployment as an inevitable problem, clearly violate these basic ethical values and priorities. There is nothing "normal" or "natural" about present unemployment rates. Indeed, massive unemployment which deprives people of the dignity of human work and an adequate family income, constitutes a social evil. It is also a major economic problem, since high unemployment rates are accompanied by lower productivity, lower consumption of products, reduced public revenues, and increasing social welfare costs. Thus, alternative strategies are required which place primary emphasis on the goals of combatting unemployment by stimulating production and permanent job creation in basic industries; developing a more balanced and equitable program for curbing inflation; and maintaining health care, social security and special assistance programs.

An alternative approach also requires that serious attention be given to the development of new industrial strategies.[23] In recent years, people have begun to raise serious questions about the desirability of economic strategies based on megaprojects, wherein large amounts of capital are invested in high-technology resource developments (e.g., large-scale nuclear plants, pipelines, hydroelectric projects). Such megaprojects may increase economic growth and profits, but they generally end up producing relatively few permanent jobs while adding to a large national debt. In our view, it is important to increase the self-sufficiency of Canada's industries, to strengthen manufacturing and construction industries, to create new job-producing industries in local communities, to redistribute capital for industrial development in underdeveloped regions and to provide relevant job-training programs.[24] It is imperative that such strategies, wherever possible, be developed on a regional basis and that labour unions and community organizations be effectively involved in their design and implementation.

6: New Directions

In order to implement these alternatives there is a need for people to take a closer look at the industrial vision and economic model that governs our society.[25] Indeed, it is becoming more evident that an industrial future is already planned by governments and corporations. According to this industrial vision, we are now preparing to move into the high-technology computer age of the 1990s.[26] In order to become more competitive in world markets, the strategy for the Eighties is to retool Canadian industries with new technologies, create new forms of high-tech industries (e.g., microelectronic, petrochemical and nuclear industries), and phase out many labour-intensive industries (e.g., textile, clothing and footwear industries). This industrial vision, in turn, is to be realized through an economic model of development that is primarily: capital intensive (using less and less human labour); energy intensive (requiring more non-renewable energy sources); foreign controlled (orienting development priorities to external interests); and export oriented (providing resources or products for markets elsewhere rather than serving basic needs of people in this country).

There are, of course, alternative ways of looking at our industrial future and organizing our economy. This does not imply a halt to technological progress but rather a fundamental reordering of the basic values and priorities of economic development. An alternative economic vision, for example, could place priority on serving the basic needs of all people in this country, on the value of human labour and on an equitable distribution of wealth and power among people and regions. What would it mean to develop an alternative economic model that would place emphasis on: socially useful forms of production; labour-intensive industries; the use of appropriate forms of technology; self-reliant models of economic development; community ownership and control of industries; new forms of worker management and ownership; and greater use of the renewable energy sources in industrial production? As a country, we have the resources, the capital, the technology and, above all else, the aspirations and skills of working men and women required to build an alternative economic future. Yet, the people of this country have seldom been challenged to envision and develop alternatives to the dominant economic model that governs our society.

At the outset, we agreed that people must indeed meet and work together as a "true community" in the face of the current economic crisis.[27] Yet, in order to forge a true community out of the present crisis, people must have a chance to choose their economic future rather than have one forced upon them. What is required, in our judgment, is a real public debate about economic visions and industrial strategies involving choices about values and priorities for the future direction of this country. Across our society, there are working and non-working people in communities—factory workers, farmers, forestry workers, miners, people on welfare, fishermen, native peoples, public service workers, and many others—who have a creative and dynamic contribution to make in shaping the economic future of our society. It is essential that serious attention be given to their concerns and proposals if the seeds of trust are to be sown for the development of a true community and a new economic order.

For our part, we will do whatever we can to stimulate public dialogue about alternative visions and strategies. More specifically, we urge local parishes or Christian communities, wherever possible, to organize public forums for discussion and debate on major issues of economic justice. Such events could provide a significant opportunity for people to discuss: (a) specific struggles of workers, the poor, and the unemployed in local communities; (b) analysis of local and regional economic problems and structures; (c) major ethical principles of economic life in the Church's recent social teachings; (d) suggestions for alternative economic visions; (e) new proposals for industrial strategies that reflect basic ethical principles. In some communities and regions, Christian groups in collaboration with other concerned groups have already launched similar events or activities for economic justice. And we encourage them to continue doing so.

Indeed, we hope and pray that more people will join in this search for alternative economic visions and strategies. For the present economic crisis, as we have seen, reveals a deepening moral disorder in the values and priorities of our society. We believe that the cries of the poor and the powerless are the voice of Christ, the Lord of History, in our midst. As Christians, we are called to become involved in struggles for economic justice and participate in the building up of a new society based on gospel principles. In so doing, we fulfill our vocation as a pilgrim people on earth, participating in Creation and preparing for the coming Kingdom.

Guidelines for Study and Action*

The long-range task of developing alternative industrial strategies requires study and action by people of good will in local and regional communities throughout this country. As a step in this direction, we encourage more local Christian communities to become involved in a process of:

- Becoming aware of the local realities and experiences of unemployment. This includes being

*(Excerpt from "Unemployment: The Human Costs," Canadian Conference of Catholic Bishops, 1980—see Appendix 4.)

present with unemployed workers, listening to their problems and identifying current and future job needs in your region.

- Analyzing the basic causes of unemployment in your region. This includes some reflection on the structural causes of unemployment to be found in our present economy, which were noted above.
- Making some ethical judgments about the realities and causes of unemployment. This includes some reflection and education on the Christian meaning of human labour and the primary goal of an economic order as serving human needs (in parishes, families, schools and community groups).
- Supporting the specific struggles of unemployed workers in your region. This includes moral and financial support for activities aimed at creating new jobs, obtaining job security for workers, planning shorter work weeks and generating public awareness about the realities and causes of unemployment.
- Participating in efforts to develop alternative industrial strategies in your region. This includes assessing the economic potential of your region, developing alternative plans for economic development and pressing local governments and corporations to change their priorities and industrial strategies.
- Increasing community ownership and control of industries where desirable. This includes the promotion of cooperatives, worker-controlled industries, and other initiatives to develop more effective community participation and control of economic life in your region.

2
The Shift in Catholic Social Teaching

Gregory Baum

Many Canadians, Catholics included, were greatly surprised by the 1983 New Year's Statement of the Canadian bishops, "Ethical Reflections on the Economic Crisis." Some thought of the Church as concerned only with eternal verities and the spiritual order, and hence were puzzled by the bishops' preoccupation with the economic crisis. Others believed that the Church was primarily concerned with personal ethics, such as contraception and abortion, and were thus taken aback by the bishops' attempt to apply moral norms to the social order. Others again associated the Church with cultural and political conservatism and were therefore astounded by the progressive, not to say left-wing, direction of the pastoral. Many Catholics were disturbed by the social teaching of their bishops. In the past, they felt, the Church had urged them to be industrious, to apply themselves and do well in the present system. Now, all of a sudden, the bishops were demanding that they become critics of the present order.

Indeed, public reaction on the whole to the bishops' statement was unusual. Previous Labour Day statements and pastoral letters, even when progressive and provocative, attracted very little attention. Yet the 1983 New Year's Statement produced a storm in the news media; and organized labour and the political parties responded vocally to the bishops' challenge. All over the country, panels and public debates were set up to deal with the meaning of the statement. In one way or another, all sectors of Canadian society became involved in the public discussion of the ecclesiastical document. What is the reason for this extraordinary phenomenon? One factor is undoubtedly the concreteness of the bishops' statement: it explicitly disagreed with government policy. But this alone does not account for the extraordinary public reaction. It can be argued that the Church document addressed the Canadian people at a moment when they were suffering from economic decline, growing unemployment, fear and uncertainty about the future, and when no other strong voice in the country helped them to analyze their plight, give them a sense of power, and point in a new direction. The Canadian bishops spoke into a void. That is why people listened. It is true, of course, that labour unions and political parties addressed themselves to some of these issues, but their approaches often reflected their own immediate institutional interests. The bishops' statement did not protect anyone's territory. It was a message of solidarity that challenged society and demanded a reply.

This commentary on the New Year's Statement will first summarize the shift to the left that has taken place in Catholic social teaching over the last decade and a half, show how this has been applied by the Canadian bishops during that time, and discuss the two fundamental ethical principles applied in the statement, namely, "the preferential option for the poor" and "the value and dignity of labour." Then the commentary will analyze the present crisis of capitalism according to these ecclesiastical documents, explore the cultural and religious meaning of the bishops' statement, examine the scope of their proposals and deal with three questions raised by their statement:

- Does it represent the arrival of a new clericalism?
- Is it rational to advocate full employment in an age of computer technology?
- Is sufficient attention given to Canada's relation to the Third World?

A Shift in Catholic Social Teaching

The *Globe and Mail* and other critical voices have suggested that the New Year's Statement is the work of a small number of bishops and represents only their own personal opinions. It is true that the statement has been produced by the eight bishops appointed to the Social Affairs Commission of the Canadian Conference of Catholic Bishops (CCCB); yet in composing the statement, the authors have been in dialogue with their fellow bishops, and the final draft was approved in principle by the executive of the CCCB. What is more important, however, is that the statement is in keeping with the shift to the left that has taken place in official Catholic social teaching over the last twelve years; and, in particular, it continues the approach taken by the Canadian bishops during that time.[1] If one overlooks this development, the bishops' statement appears simply as a flash in the pan. In fact, it is the fruit of an emerging social theory that has evolved in the social messages and pastoral letters of the Canadian bishops.

The synthesis of social ideals, called "Catholic social teaching," originated at the end of the nineteenth century with Pope Leo XIII, who brought together the reformist ideas of the Catholic social activists of the time.[2] Subsequent popes have endorsed this teaching. Society, according to the teaching, is an organic reality, a body, based on cooperation and hierarchy, that must constantly be reformed through the submission of all to the norms of justice. It is the task of the government to stand above the conflict of the classes, promote the common good of society and protect the poor against exploitation by the rich. Catholic social teaching resembled the old British "Tory" social philosophy that survived in Canada among the so-called radical Tories.[3] Catholic social teaching defended private property (and hence opposed socialism) and supported the unionization of labour (and hence opposed economic liberalism). While this teaching had strong reformist impulses, its main emphasis was on the organic unity of society, on cooperation, on shared values and on respect for authority. The struggle for justice had to take place within this social context.

It was in Latin America in the Sixties that Catholic social teaching abandoned this organic understanding of society. Christian grass-roots movements proposed that the Latin American countries were caught in the clutches of a system that impoverished them, that they were prisoners of world capitalism, that the decisions that affected production and distribution in their countries were made in the head offices of the large transnational corporations, usually in the United States, by men whose aim was simply to increase corporate profit and power. Even the development projects sponsored by the capitalist nations increased the dependency and eventually the misery of Latin America. Only members of a small class of Latin Americans, linked to the transnational corporations, greatly improved their standard of living and for that reason became the political actors in these countries whose interest lay in protecting the existing order. In this situation it was impossible to think of society in organic terms. What was required was a conflictual approach. To gain an appropriate understanding of these countries, it was necessary to analyze the structures of oppression. The Christian radicals, together with their secular comrades, envisaged a society defined by self-reliant economic development that made use of local resources and the skills available among the people, and produced the food, the goods and the services that the people needed. They called this liberation.

In 1968 the Latin American bishops conference at Medellin accepted this liberationist perspective in some of their documents.[4] They replaced the organic approach to society by a conflictual one. They recognized that their countries were caught in structures of dependency or colonialism. They distinguished between "external colonialism," defined by economic dependency on transnational corporations and foreign governments, and "internal colonialism," defined by the oppressive and rigid class structure, in particular by the new middle class that benefited from the presence of world capitalism. What Christian faith required, according to the Medellin documents, was solidarity with the masses of the poor and dispossessed. The bishops argued that fidelity to Jesus Christ demanded solidarity with the poor. As we shall see, the next Latin American bishops conference at Puebla (1979) endorsed and strengthened this approach.

This new social teaching influenced what was happening at the Vatican, the centre of the Catholic Church. In 1971 two ecclesiastical documents were published that adopted the new liberationist perspective. First, the letter *Octogesima Adveniens*, written by Pope Paul VI to the Cardinal Archbishop of Quebec, Maurice Roy, at that time president of the Justice and Peace Commission, broke new ground. First, it removed the taboo from socialism.[5] It acknowledged that many Catholics had become socialists because their Christian convictions led them to this. The letter recognized several forms of socialism and warned against a socialism that was wedded to a total philosophy. The same letter also introduced a more nuanced approach to Marxism.[6] Paul VI distinguished between Marxism as a total world view and Marxism as a form of political organization, both of which he repudiated. But if Marxism is understood as a form of social analysis, as a sociology of oppression, then, according to Paul VI, it can be very useful in the struggle for justice, as long as it is applied with care and one avoids the temptation of explaining the whole of culture in terms of the economic infrastructure. This cautious recommendation was later endorsed by several episcopal conferences, including the Canadian bishops'.

Octogesima Adveniens (n. 37) praised the emergence of "utopia" in social theory. This "utopia" did not mean the dream of a perfect society, removed from the possibilities of present history, a never-never land of social concord; what was meant, rather, in accord with the social thought of the German revisionist Marxist philosopher, Ernst Bloch, was utopia as the vision of an alternative society, in discontinuity with the status quo, yet close enough to the as yet unrealized possibilities of the present that it could generate imaginative political strategies and release energy for the social struggle. This orientation towards utopia broke the organicist imagination, until then predominant in Catholic social theory, which regarded reform as a kind of restoration of a more just or more humane society belonging to the past. Utopia, as defined in *Octogesima Adveniens*, has been operative in the emerging Canadian Catholic social theory, in particular the 1983 New Year's Statement.

In the same year, 1971, the Second Synod of Bishops, meeting in Rome, promulgated the document *Justitia in Mundo*, which adopted a conflictual approach to the understanding of society and a liberationist perspective in the proclamation of the Gospel.[7] What is demanded today, the document claims, is a global analysis of economic and political forces. No society can any longer be understood simply by itself. On the global scale, *Justitia in Mundo* perceives an expanding system of dependency and oppression, which draws the smaller nations, especially the former colonies, into greater subservience to the large economic corporations. It also acknowledges the struggles of peoples, groups and classes to free themselves from domination and assume responsibility for themselves. The bishops declare themselves in solidarity with the oppressed and marginalized struggling for justice. In *Justitia in Mundo* emerges a principle that would eventually be called "the option for the poor." Only through solidarity with the people struggling for justice will the Church be able to unfold its social message.

It is of interest to us that Canadian bishops made a significant contribution to the 1971 Synod of Bishops. The Canadian position was presented by Cardinal Flahiff, then archbishop of Winnipeg.[8] In a now famous speech, he proposed that the Church's traditional social teaching has had little impact because it was abstract and academic, removed from people's historical struggles. "I suggest that, henceforth, our basic principle must be: only knowledge gained through participation is valid in this area of justice. True knowledge can be gained only through concern and solidarity." He then added, "Unless we are in solidarity with the people who are poor, marginal, or isolated we cannot even speak effectively about their problems." This approach has characterized the teaching of the Canadian bishops ever since.

The 1971 Synod of Bishops also worked out a renewed understanding of the Church's mission in society. Why should the Church be concerned about justice? Cardinal Flahiff had already brought up this question in his presentation. He had given this reply: "The Christian message liberates. It liberates from sin—not only from personal sin, but also and perhaps chiefly from social sin, since social sin, like original sin, creates a situation where individual sin becomes easy and acceptable." Social sin, in the context, refers to social structures that cause oppression and exploitation. The synod fully endorsed this position. Basing itself on the new Latin American approach, seconded by other episcopal conferences, such as the Canadian, the synod endorsed the liberationist perspective. In the final statement, *Justitia in Mundo*, we are told that the proclamation of the Gospel includes active witness to human rights and social justice, that the Church's mission to promote the Gospel includes engagement in the struggle for justice, and that the redemption which Jesus Christ has brought includes the liberation of people from the oppressive conditions of their lives. The synod, thus, records an important development in Catholic doctrine.

The year 1971 was a turning point in the Catholic Church's official teaching. The organicist perspective was left behind in favour of a conflictual approach to society. Society is now viewed as being made up of dominant structures and countervailing trends. This new approach has been fully endorsed by Pope John Paul II's pivotal encyclical *Laborem Exencens* (1981). Here the Pope designates as the dynamic element of modern society the workers' struggle for social justice. He calls for the solidarity *of* workers and *with* workers.[9] Extending this principle to Third World societies, he calls for the solidarity *of* the poor and *with* the poor, and insists that the Church itself must join this movement. Fidelity to Jesus Christ commits the Church to political witness.

Catholic Social Theory in Canada

An important development in Catholic social theory has taken place in Canada. It should be said immediately that in Canada this evolution has occurred on an ecumenical basis. Since the late Sixties, Canadian churches have cooperated in the area of social justice. On many occasions they have spoken in one voice. The churches have been willing to sponsor and support several interchurch committees, whose task it has been to examine various social and economic issues from a Christian liberationist perspective. At the same time, many small Christian communities have been operative in Canada, some Catholic, some Protestant and some ecumenical, dedicated to particular social justice struggles. They have existed among factory workers in Quebec, among Native Peoples in the North, among the welfare poor in cities and the country, among poor immigrants and political refugees. This network of groups and centres, linked to the officially supported interchurch committees, has constituted a significant minority movement in the Christian churches. For Protestants, this has represented the return to an earlier tradition, the social gospel, the religion of social involvement in the earlier part of this century.[10] For Catholics, it has meant the emergence of new, prophetic Catholicism, closely linked to the worldwide social justice movement in the Church. Church leaders have taken this movement seriously. It was out of dialogue with this movement and in reliance on the development in the World Church that the Canadian Catholic bishops produced their important social justice statements in the Seventies and early Eighties.

The most important of these statements are the following: "Northern Development: At What Cost?" (1975), "From Words to Action" (1976), "A Society to Be Transformed" (1977), "Unemployment: The Human Costs" (1980) and, finally, the January 1983 statement, "Ethical Reflections on the Economic Crisis." The statements prior to 1983 are reprinted as appendixes in this book.*

The following paragraphs summarize some of the significant positions adopted by the Canadian bishops.[11] It will become quite clear that their 1983 statement on the economic crisis was the result of their sustained reflection over the years. In the 1976 Labour Day Statement, "From Words to Action," the bishops recognize that something is seriously amiss in society.

> Many people agree that there is something wrong with the present social and economic order. It fails to meet the human needs of the majority of the people. The present economic order results in a very uneven distribution of wealth and the control of resources by a small minority. On the global scene, the poor peoples, especially in the Third World, are calling for the creation of a new economic order based on a just distribution of wealth and power. And within this country, in its various regions and communities, there are similar signs that people want to find new approaches, to make better use of human and material resources, and to end waste and want and exploitation. (n. 3)

What ought to be the Christian reaction to this? The 1976 Labour Day Statement has this to say: "As disciples of Christ, all of us have a special responsibility to play a role in the creation of a

---

*Quotations from and references to the documents in the appendixes will be identified by the numbered paragraphs in which they are found.

social order based on justice. For we stand in the biblical tradition of the prophets of Israel where to know God is to seek justice for the disinherited, the poor and the oppressed" (n. 4). The bishops add, "For the Christian community this struggle for justice is not an optional activity: it is integral to bringing the Gospel to the world" (n. 5). In their own words, the Canadian bishops here restate the teaching of the 1971 Synod of Bishops that the Church's mission includes witness to justice and action to transform society.

In the same document the bishops recognize the grass-roots movement for social justice in the Church, and acknowledge its ecumenical character. "A variety of Christian groups have been working with the poor and oppressed peoples of their communities, organizing educational events on issues of injustice, and pressing leaders of government and industries to change policies that cause human suffering" (n. 7). The bishops recognize that those who are committed to this Christian way of life are presently "a minority" in the Church, but they call them "a significant minority" because their witness challenges the entire Church to greater fidelity.

What are Christians to do? "From Words to Action" outlines several steps (n. 9). These steps are of interest to us, since in writing their 1983 statement on the economic crisis, the bishops have followed them. Among the necessary steps are:

- *Christians must reread the Scriptures to hear in them God's call to justice*. This step reveals that the commitment to social justice is a spiritual event. As we shall see further on, the Christian struggle for social justice is not "activitism"; it includes faith and the transformation of consciousness.

- *Christians must listen to the victims of society*. If middle-class people only speak to one another, they acquire a distorted picture of society. They do not become aware of the contradictions of the present order. Canadians easily get the impression that oppressed people exist in Third World countries but not in Canada. The bishops argue, however, that Canadians will acquire "a new vision of reality by becoming more present to the hungry, the homeless, the jobless, the native person, the poor immigrant and others who may be victims of injustices in our communities."
- *Christians must speak out against injustices.* Silence amounts to approval of what is happening. As citizens we must exercise our freedom and speak out against the causes of injustice. Christian social justice groups have in fact worked with several oppressed groups in Canadian society and manifested their solidarity in political witness and action.[12]
- *Christians must analyze the causes of injustice and join others in the struggle to remove these causes from society*. What is implied in this step is, first, that injustices have causes that can be analyzed with the help of social science. We must try to identify the structural causes of oppression. This steps implies, secondly, that these causes are not connatural to society, demanding our resigned acceptance. They are symptoms of irrationality that can be overcome in a joint struggle.

In their 1983 statement on the economic crisis,

the Canadian bishops followed these four steps very carefully. They began with the spiritual message, "the option for the poor," derived from the Scriptures; they then examined Canadian society from the viewpoint of the unemployed and low-income people; they denounced present government policies as a source of injustice; and they analyzed the structural causes of the present crisis and recommended solidarity with other Canadians in the struggle for an alternative society.

The 1977 Labour Day Statement, "A Society to Be Transformed," made important contributions to the emerging Catholic social theory. The points of note in the commentary are those that anticipate the bishops' approach in the 1983 New Year's Statement. In what direction, the 1977 Labour Day Statement asks, shall concerned Catholics move Canadian society? The statement repudiates the two opposing ideologies of liberal capitalism and Marxist collectivism (nn. 13-16). They reject, in line with traditional Catholic teaching, an economic system that makes the market the unique instrument for promoting production and distributing wealth; and they condemn the Marxist system which looks upon people only in terms of their economic function and thus absorbs their individual freedoms in a collectivist order. The presentation of Catholic social teaching as "a third way" between economic liberalism and Marxist collectivism has been common in the Church. But to understand what this means, we have to take a closer look at the various ways in which this term has been used.

From Leo XIII's *Rerum Novarum* (1891) to Pius XI's *Quadragesimo Anno* (1931), Catholic social teaching was presented as a middle way between capitalism and socialism. Following a corporatist imagination, the papal documents held up an idealized vision of feudal society, where the government is thought to protect and promote the common good, defend private property on the one hand, yet on the other control the use of capital for the benefit of all. Government is to be carried on by high-minded men who stand above the conflict of the classes. After the Second World War, Catholic social teaching, with the support of Pius XII, became more affirmative in regard to democracy, pluralism, industrialization and other features of modern society. Now "the third way" between liberalism and socialism came to be defined in a new manner. The social program recommended by Catholic social teaching is embodied in the newly found Christian Democratic parties in countries such as Italy and Germany and in particular in South and Central America.[13] These parties advocated a restrained capitalism, that is, a mixed capitalist economy under the guidance of a strong government and strengthened by progressive labour legislation. To this day, the Christian Democratic parties in Latin America refer to themselves as "the third way."

The liberation movements in Latin America repudiate this third way. They argue that in the long run this alternative always becomes a defence of the world capitalist order. They favour, instead, a self-reliant, socialist economy, in relative independence of the First World nations. Yet in their own manner the Latin American liberation movements also advocate a third way, somewhere between capitalism and Marxism, an alternative to be defined by their ongoing experience.

What follows from this brief account is that whenever the term "third way" is used, one must carefully analyze what precisely it refers to. When the 1977 Labour Day Statement presents the emerging Catholic social theory as a third way, does it recommend the return to the old corporatist teaching? The answer is negative. The 1977 Labour Day Statement has thoroughly assimilated the social position of Paul VI's *Octogesima Adveniens*, mentioned above. In particular, the Canadian 1977 statement includes socialism as a viable option for Catholics; it recommends the careful use of a Marxist sociology of oppression; and it opts not for restoration but for utopia, in the sense which the secular philosopher Ernst Bloch and Pope Paul VI gave to this term.

In what direction, then, will Canadian Catholics move when they commit themselves to social justice? They may not always be united in the same political project. The Canadian bishops again refer to *Octogesima Adveniens*, which recognized that Catholics committed to justice often disagree among themselves on what political movement demands their loyalty. Despite these differences, *Octogesima Adveniens* (n. 50) urged that Catholics remain friends in Jesus Christ. The 1977 Labour Day Statement (n. 18) says that some Catholics committed to social justice believe that the capitalist system can be reformed in accordance with appropriate ethical ideals; other Catholics, it says, have despaired over capitalism and have joined a socialist project, which they try to reconcile with the spirit of Jesus. Finally, some Christians, it says, accept neither of these two options and struggle for a socio-economic order beyond them. What does this third option refer to? The bishops may have been thinking of the cooperative movement that operates out of a theory critical of both capitalism and socialism, especially of a centralizing socialism based on state ownership of industry. The bishops may also have thought of the ecological movement. Critical of capitalism and socialism, which are both growth oriented, the ecological movement worries about the protection of the earth's surface, the destruction of nature and the exhaustion of natural resources. It advocates slow growth, the use of renewable energy, and new strategies for the production of goods and the improvement of human lifestyles. The Canadian bishops may also have thought of Catholic social movements, such as Catholic Worker, founded in the U.S. by Dorothy Day and Peter Maurin, which distrust all giant organizations, including government and political parties, and put their trust into the reconstruction of society from below, through the creation of small communities operating out of countercultural gospel principles.[14]

According to the 1977 Labour Day Statement, Catholics dedicated to social justice may be found in a variety of movements. The bishops plead that despite these differences, they remain friends in Jesus Christ, respect one another and strengthen the bond of peace among them.

We notice in the 1977 Labour Day Statement a trait that is also found in the other statements made by the Canadian bishops, including the 1983 New Year's Statement. The social messages of the bishops can be read in several ways; in particular, they can be read in a reformist and a more radical manner. "Reformist" refers to improving or rectifying the existing order, while "radical" here refers to the creation of an alternative society. In this context, it is useful to introduce the following distinction. A reformist proposal may be of two kinds: it may aim at the reform of the present system in order to make it function more efficiently and hence give it greater stability (this could be called "reformist reform"); or a reformist proposal may aim at the reform of the present system through the introduction of a new principle which, in the long run, will reveal itself as antithetical to the present order and thus initiate a more radical transformation of society (this may be called "system-transcending reform"). A good example of the latter is the cooperative movement. It presents itself as a reform project; it does not wrestle against the existing capitalist order, but once introduced, it reveals itself as operating out of a principle at odds with capitalism, namely, cooperative ownership; and if it does not become adapted to capitalism, as is usually the case,[15] it will initiate people to critical consciousness and prepare a more radical transformation of society.

In 1980 the Canadian bishops published a social message entitled "Unemployment: The Human Costs." This document presented an analysis of the causes of unemployment (nn. 7-9). Its recommendations, as we shall see, anticipated the proposals of the 1983 New Year's Statement. In their 1980 social message, the bishops lament the high rate of unemployment in Canada. They argue that the human costs of unemployment are enormous—personal hardship, mental anxiety, strain on family life, conflicts, depression and sometimes even suicide. It is of utmost importance, the bishops say, to analyze the causes of unemployment. Why? Because if we do not, we are tempted to put the blame on the innocent and the victims. In their ignorance, some people blame the workers for the present crisis: they supposedly ask for excessive wages. Some people blame women for unemployment: they should stay at home instead of taking jobs away from men. Others blame the immigrants, especially the visible minorities: they are taking the jobs of Canadians. These false attributions of blame have dangerous social consequences. They legitimate class oppression, sexism and racism. It is imperative, therefore, to look for the true causes of the present crisis.

To what causes do the bishops attribute present unemployment in Canada? The present deindustrialization, they argue, is the result of the changing structure of capital in this country. How has capitalism changed in Canada? The message first mentions "the concentration" of capital: this refers to the growth of corporations, the enlargement of their power, and the small elite that is responsible for decision making. Since members of this largely anonymous elite do not share residential areas with the workers and hence are not linked to them as members of the same community, they view the needs of Canadian workers in the abstract, and the decisions they make simply aim at the maximization of profit and power. Second, the social message speaks of "the centralization" of capital. This refers to the concentration of the major industrial, commercial and financial institutions in the metropolitan areas of Canada that leads to a growing regional disparity and an uneven spread of unemployment. Third, the social message mentions the "high level of foreign ownership" of Canada's principal industries. The important decisions regarding production and employment are made by people outside the country who have no interest in the well-being of Canadian workers. An economic crisis in the United States results in the speedy shutdown of Canadian branch plants. (The 1983 New Year's Statement adds to this "the internationalization" of capital: this refers to the power of the transnational corporations, whether their head office is in Canada or in some other country, to shift capital and entire units of production to parts of the world where labour is cheaper and hence profits higher, where underpaid workers are not organized, and where, in many instances, military governments prevent them from creating labour unions.) The 1980 social message then mentions the orientation of the Canadian economy towards "the export of natural resources" with limited opportunities of employment, while what the country needs is a more developed manufacturing sector. The message also mentions the trend towards ever more "capital-intensive industries," either through the new computer technology or the concentration of megaprojects, unconcerned about the impact on Canadian workers. Finally, the message refers to "the prolongation of lockouts and strikes, which result in a loss of productivity and aggravate conditions of unemployment."

Already in this 1980 social message, the Canadian bishops speak of unemployment in Canada as a social evil (n. 10). They quote Pope John Paul II's statement that "the plague of unemployment" is symptomatic of a basic moral disorder. The bishops' message says, "The primary purpose of any economic system, the Church has consistently taught, should be to serve the basic needs required by all people for a more fully human life" (n. 11). The bishops then ask these questions:

> As a modern capitalist society, have we reached the point where greater priority is placed on the value of machines rather than on the value of human labour? Where maximizing profits and growth takes precedence over the goal of serving real human needs? Where protecting private property exists to the detriment of the right to work for thousands of people? (n. 12)

Earlier Catholic social teaching suggests that these questions have not suddenly emerged in the present crisis; they deserved to be asked of the capitalist economy from the beginning.[16]

"As Christians," the 1980 social message tells us, "we have an alternative vision" of society. "This vision includes a more equitable redistribution of wealth and power among all the people and the development of this country's resources to serve basic human needs" (n. 13). Already in this document, the alternative model of economic development is defined as requiring: "effective measures to increase the self-sufficiency of Canada's industries, strengthen the manufacturing sector and other job-producing industries, redistribute capital for industrial development in underdeveloped regions and enhance community ownership and control of local industries" (n. 14). The statement of 1980 leads directly to the New Year's Statement of 1983. There is perfect continuity in the emerging Canadian Catholic social theory.

The Preferential Option for the Poor

The New Year's Statement of 1983* recognizes the extent of the economic decline in Canada and the devastating consequences this has had on vast numbers of people. It mentions plant shutdowns, massive layoffs, wage-restraint programs, suspension of collective bargaining, abandoned one-industry towns, depleting unemployment insurance benefits, cutbacks in health and social services, and personal consequences such as anxiety, tension in the family, despair and sometimes even suicide. Our economy is in trouble, the bishops conclude.

The statement argues that the burden of the economic decline has been placed on the backs of the people who can least defend themselves: the workers, the unemployed, people living on low incomes. The federal wage-restraint program is divisive and unjust because it is not accompanied by an equivalent restraint program for prices and profits. What Canadian society experiences at this time is not simply the technical failure of an economic system, but a moral disorder as well. For this reason, ethical reflections on the present economic crisis are imperative. The bishops argue that operative in the present economic policies are priorities and values that are quite unacceptable. What is required is a shift to a new ethical perspective. What the country needs are economic policies that operate out of values, and protect priorities, that promote the well-being of the people.

*The 1983 statement, printed in the front of this volume, does not have numbered paragraphs. Quotations from it will be identified by the numbered sections, s. 1 to s. 6, in which they are found.

Economics and ethics are intertwined. Some economists object to such a philosophical position. They want economics to be a value-free objectivist science. This issue will be examined further on. For the bishops, the separation of economics and ethics would spell the end of our civilization.

What are the ethical principles in the light of which the bishops examine the existing economic policies? They are two in particular: "the preferential option for the poor" and "the value and dignity of labour" (s. 1). What precisely these principles mean shall become clear in the following discourse.

What is "the option for the poor"? It can be said that the Christian church has always preached an option for the poor by calling upon people to be compassionate and to assist those who suffer from hunger and misery. The option for the poor has also had an ascetical meaning in the Catholic tradition. Many Christians, especially the religious orders, believed that by living in simplicity and even in voluntary poverty, they became more open to the Divine Spirit, more faithful disciples of Jesus and more closely bound to their brothers and sisters. In the Latin American Catholic Church, in particular in the documents of the Puebla Conference (1979), the preferential option for the poor has acquired a clearly defined socio-political meaning.[17] The option for the poor in this instance means solidarity with the oppressed and the willingness to look at one's own society from their viewpoint. The preferential option for the poor includes social commitment and entry into a new consciousness. In the language of contemporary Catholic theology, the option is a "praxis": it begins with commitment, which in turn affects how reality is perceived, which in turn leads to further action, and so forth, the entire interaction aiming at the liberation of people from oppression.

The option for the poor, according to the Puebla Conference, is based on God's Word in the Scriptures. Solidarity with the oppressed has been revealed in Exodus in the liberation of the people of Israel from the power of Pharaoh; it was emphasized in the Torah, the Law of Moses, which expressed God's special care for the poor, the helpless and the unprotected; it was reinforced by the Hebrew prophets who condemned exploitation and announced that to know God was to seek justice for the disinherited and oppressed; it was confirmed through the coming of Jesus Christ, who stood in solidarity with the poor of his day, who announced God's blessing on those who hunger and thirst after justice, and who was himself persecuted as a troublemaker by the religious establishment and later condemned to be crucified by the imperial authorities, the punishment reserved for rebels and insurgents. The option for the poor was endorsed in Christ's resurrection, the divine pledge that all the humiliated people of the world will be vindicated. The murderers shall not remain victorious over their innocent victims.

In liberation theology and in several ecclesiastical texts, the option for the poor is presented as a dimension of the Christian faith. It is not a secular, but a specifically religious, commitment. This raises the difficult question of how it is possible to recommend the option for the poor as a principle applicable to society as a whole, made up as it is of people who largely define themselves in secular terms.

Traditional Catholic social teaching did not invoke the Scriptures; it relied instead on natural law imperatives, that is to say, on ethical reflections, based on universal reason, claiming validity for believers and non-believers alike. Catholic social teaching then clearly distinguished between the order of reason and the order of revelation. Pope John XXIII's encyclical *Mater et Magistra* (1961) is perhaps the first major ecclesiastical document in which Jesus Christ is named as the inspirer and guarantor of the Church's social teaching. Natural reason and Christian wisdom are intertwined. People who wrestle with issues of justice and truth are not simply left to their own limited resources, but God's grace is operative among them. God is graciously present to human history. The God of biblical revelation is not conceived of as above history, ruling the world from on high, but as in and through history, empowering and enlightening people in their quest for justice and truth. Seeing the world in this perspective, Catholics hold that the social principles derived from the Scriptures are not at odds with the aspirations of humanity, but rather in keeping with them. The biblical imperatives are a scandal to a human reason that is distorted by the dominant ideology, but they are in accord with the deepest level of practical reason, reaching out towards the emancipation of human life.

The option for the poor, then, can be defended not only by an appeal to the teaching of the Bible but also by an application of practical reason. This commentary is not the place to examine this important ethical issue, but it is worth noting that this principle of practical reason was first formulated in

Hegel's *Phenomenology of the Spirit*, where it was shown that the master/servant relationship damaged not only the humanity of the slave, but also that of the master. Oppression damages the oppressed but also harms the oppressors. The misfortune of the subjugated becomes the misfortune of the whole society. Only through solidarity with the victims do we gain a truthful understanding of society, and only then can we initiate a process destined to overcome the injustices inflicted on people, and transcend the corresponding distortion of culture as a whole.

The option for the poor, in the precise meaning given to it by the Puebla Conference, expresses the commitment to look upon one's society from the viewpoint of the oppressed and marginalized (the epistemological dimension) and to give public witness to solidarity with the poor (the activist dimension). We note that this option is a critical principle that retains its validity in, through and beyond any revolutionary change. Through historical transformations, new elites will emerge and new groups of people may find themselves excluded, marginalized and oppressed. The ongoing "option for the poor" will allow Christians to remain critical and, from within the social commitment, to make moral demands on the liberation movements during and after their social struggle. In this it differs from the preferential option for a nation or the preferential option for the proletariat, made in abstraction from the actual role and location of these groups in history, options that easily lead to an uncritical glorification of these groups and then become stances akin to idolatry. The option for the poor is a critical principle of transcendent dimension.

The option for the poor, as formulated at the Puebla Conference, was endorsed in Pope John Paul II's encyclical, *Laborem Exercens*. As noted earlier, the Pope argues that the dynamic element of modern society is the workers' struggle for social justice, a struggle that must be joined by all who love justice, including the Church itself. The encyclical calls for "solidarity *of* workers and *with* workers" (n. 8). In a subsequent paragraph, extending this reasoning to Third World nations, the Pope calls for "the solidarity *of* the poor and *with* the poor." Solidarity here is partial or preferential. As the ultimate aim, the Church proclaims universal solidarity with the whole human family; but in order to create the historical conditions for such a solidarity in a world marked by oppression, solidarity must first be extended to the victims. It must be preferential; it must embrace the poor rather than the rich, and the powerless rather than the powerful. While in this sinful world solidarity must remain preferential, its ultimate purpose is the creation of a truly universal solidarity.

In their statement on the economic crisis, the Canadian bishops call the option for the poor the first principle of their critical reflections. They look upon Canada from the viewpoint of the people at the base and in the margin, that is, through the eyes of all who suffer from structural injustices. The bishops reject the economic policies that define Canadian society at this time because these policies disfavour workers, the unemployed and low-income people. The principle of solidarity that the bishops invoke demands a preferential loyalty to the underprivileged and exploited, in view of creating a society in which solidarity achieves truly universal dimensions. "This option," the bishops write, "calls for economic policies which realize that the needs of the poor have priority over the wants of the rich; that the rights of the workers are more important than the maximization of profit; that the participation of marginalized groups has precedence over the preservation of the system which excludes them" (s. 1).

The Value and Dignity of Labour

The second moral principle invoked by the bishops' statement is called "the value and dignity of labour." This is an ancient biblical principle, in the name of which the Christian church has always honoured peasants, craftsmen, labourers and later industrial workers, even when these were despised by the powerful in society. In Catholic social teaching, however, "the value and dignity of labour" gradually acquired a more technical meaning. The principle meant that workers, because of the value and dignity of labour, have the right to share in the decisions affecting the work process and the use of the product of their work. Pius XI (1922-39) was the first pope to recommend that workers share in the ownership and management of the industries. "In the present state of society, it is advisable that the wage contract be modified somewhat by a contract of partnership. For thus the workers and executives become sharers in the ownership or management, or else participate in some way in the profits."[18] In John Paul II's *Laborem Exercens* the principle is greatly enhanced and extended. "When man works, using all the means of production, he also wishes the fruit of this work to be used by himself and others, and he wishes to be able to take part in the very work process as a sharer in responsib creativity at the workbench to which he ap himself" (n. 15). Because of the value and dignity labour, we are told, workers are co-responsible for the management of the industries and for the use to which capital and surplus value are put. Ultimately, John Paul II argues (n. 14), the workers should be the owners of the giant workbench, the industries, at which they labour.

In the same encyclical, *Laborem Exercens*, "the value and dignity of labour" has become a critical principle, in the light of which the work done by people—in other words, the entire economy—must be evaluated. To what extent do industrial processes and economic policies damage the value and dignity of labour? The encyclical argues that whenever decisions regarding work and workers are made by a type of reasoning that only aims at the technological perfection of the industries and the increase of profit for the owners, the workers are robbed of their dignity and treated as objects or commodities. We need industrial institutions and economic policies that allow workers to remain subjects. Secondly, the encyclical argues that whenever capital and surplus value are used against the interests of the workers who have produced them, we have a violation of the priority of labour over capital. The priority of labour over capital, the central phrase of the entire encyclical, affirms that capital must be used in the service of labour; that is, it must serve the labourers employed in the industry, serve the renewal of the productive machinery and finally serve the entire labouring society.[19]

The Canadian bishops make ample reference to

the value and dignity of labour. They argue that the present economic policy in fact violates this principle. They refer more specifically to John Paul II's rephrasing of this principle as "the priority of labour over capital." In the present crisis, the bishops argue, there is a new attempt, in violation of a previous social consensus, to make capital again the dominant organizing principle of economic life. "By placing greater importance on the accumulation of profits and machines than on the people who work in a given economy, the value, meaning and dignity of human labour is violated" (s. 3). The bishops argue that the present plans for the economic recovery of Canada make great economic concessions to private ownership in the hope that the ingenuity and resourcefulness of the capitalist class will reconstruct Canada's industrial base. The bishops think that such hopes are illusory. "For even if companies recover and increase their profit margins, the additional revenues are likely to be reinvested in some labour-saving technology, exported to other countries or spent on market speculation or luxury goods" (s. 4). While it is absolutely necessary to develop the industrial sectors of the Canadian economy, especially the production of goods, the attempt to do this along lines that simply promote capital and extend technology will inevitably lead to greater unemployment and to conditions of labour for those who are employed that diminish their dignity. "As long as technology and capital are not harnassed by society to serve basic human needs, they are likely to become an enemy rather than an ally in the development of peoples" (s. 3).

The basic conflict in society, according to

Laborem Exercens and the Canadian statement, is between workers and capital that is organized against them. Archbishop Ted Scott, the Anglican primate of Canada, in his personal response—a response that was on the whole positive—suggested that the Catholic bishops' statement was ambiguous and could lead to misunderstandings. When John Paul II spoke of labourers, he included not only industrial workers but scientists, technical experts, service workers as well as managers, while the New Year's Statement, following a narrower definition of labour, seems to put labour always in opposition to management. The Catholic bishops' statement, Archbishop Scott thought, has a combative note that is absent from *Laborem Exercens*. The difference between the two ecclesiastical documents, however, is more apparent than real. It is true that in *Laborem Exercens*, John Paul II counts as belonging to labour manual and nonmanual workers, including people working in management. While he takes the metaphor for the human vocation from the working class—he defines man as worker—he extends the meaning of work to include all the contributions people make to the building of society. Society itself is conceived of as labouring. According to John Paul II, the conflict in this society is not between workers and managers, nor even necessarily between workers and capital, but between workers and capital organized against them to increase the power and profit of the controlling class. The Pope believes that while labour and capital are meant to be united and in harmony, the actual organization of capital against labour at the beginning of industrial capitalism created the conditions for the opposition between them. He writes: "The conflict originated in the fact that the workers put their powers at the disposal of the entrepreneurs, and these, following the principle of maximum profit, tried to establish the lowest possible wages for the work done by the employees" (n. 11). Whether those working in management are counted among the workers or identified with capital depends largely on their own decisions. The Pope's call for the solidarity *of* workers and *with* workers applies also to them.

In keeping with *Laborem Exercens*, the New Year's Statement opposes an economy that makes capital the dominating organizing principle. Yet it makes no suggestion that in every single dispute labour is right and management is wrong. The statement acknowledges that "limited perspectives and excessive demands" can also be found among labour unions (s. 1). The labour struggle in a particular industry must be interpreted, according to the statement, in the context of the wider struggle for the priority of labour over capital in the Canadian economy. With this principle, as we shall see, the statement also challenges the labour movement.

A second objection to the New Year's Statement, made by several members of Parliament, is that the priority of labour over capital is a principle of Marxist origin. It is therefore useful in this commentary to distinguish the Catholic position from that of official Marxism, without examining the question whether there are revisionist Marxist theories that actually resemble the teaching of *Laborem Exercens*. According to this Marxism, the origin of exploitation resided in private ownership: the owner of the industry was able to appropriate the goods produced by the workers he employed. For Marx this was expropriation or theft. According to the Catholic theory, the ownership question is not crucial. Ownership may be private (*Laborem Exercens* still defends the right of private property) or it may be in various ways social or public; what is more significant in all these cases is the *use* of capital.[20] How is capital and profit employed? If private ownership aims at maximizing profit, it becomes a source of exploitation. Yet state ownership offers no guarantee that capital and profit will be used to serve labour. While public ownership is often a necessity, it may produce as exploitative an economy as private ownership. It is only the participation of workers in decisions affecting the economy that can offer some guarantee that the priority of labour over capital will be protected. Catholic social theory thus advocates the co-responsibility of workers and local communities in determining the use of capital and profits. This principle, it should be noted, is critical of capitalism as well as communism. It cautions against any kind of centralizing socialism that advocates the nationalization of all industrial, commercial and financial institutions. What the Catholic principle stands for is the entry of democracy into the planning and organization of production.

A Structural Crisis of Capitalism

According to the New Year's Statement, the present economic decline is related to a much larger structural crisis of international capitalism (s. 2). Two historical factors in particular are mentioned: the internationalization of capital and the introduction of new computer technology. Both lead to a reorganization of the economy. In particular they lead to deindustrialization in the developed countries, to permanent, structural unemployment, and thus to the marginalization of widening sectors of the population. Even military arms production, which during the Second World War created employment at home and aided economic recovery, today introduces labour-saving, capital-intensive technology—and thus only intensifies the economic crisis. There are signs that there is enough finance capital in the world, the New Year's Statement says, but banks and other financial institutions prefer to wait for a more profitable investment climate. Under these conditions, governments find themselves obliged to create favourable conditions for private investment, which include wage-restraint programs, cutbacks in social services, and new legislation that limits the power gained by labour unions. While New Deal capitalism recognized the needs of society as a whole and hence supported the national welfare state, at least to some extent, the present crisis undermines this social consensus. The giant corporations acting on the world scale no longer assume responsibility for the nation in which their head office is located. The ideal of full employment and public welfare, which had been endorsed by governments since the New Deal (in Canada since the Second World War), has been gradually abandoned.

The position adopted by the Canadian bishops assumes its full meaning only when placed in the historical picture drawn by Pope John Paul II in *Laborem Exercens*. In this encyclical John Paul II identifies two phases of capitalism and argues that a new, third phase is about to begin, one that is characterized by great brutality—unless it can be stopped.[21] The first phase was entrepreneurial, free-enterprise capitalism, based on family-owned companies, that was revolutionary in character and created the conditions of modern society. It undermined the old feudal order; it fostered democratic governments; it created previously unheard-of wealth; it fostered science and technology; and it created a new, secular cultural climate in which personal ambition and resourcefulness were the great virtues. The early capitalism operated out of a liberal ideology that made personal freedom the great ideal. At the same time it created the industrial working class under conditions of grave oppression. Capitalism was the source of enormous suffering. The free-enterprise philosophy, John Paul II thinks, allowed the early capitalists to organize their ever-growing capital against the workers. He speaks here of "rigid capitalism." Out of the enormous hardship of nineteenth-century Europe, soon followed by hardship in America, burst forth a movement of "labour solidarity" that was to have great influence on Western history.

Thanks to the impact of the labour movement and the support it received from progressive governments, and because of other factors pertaining to the growth of industries, capitalism entered upon a second phase. This was true at least for the Western nations. The family-owned companies gave way to larger corporations, owned by shareholders, run by managers and controlled by an elite. These corporations recognized their dependence on the cooperation of society. Society trained workers for them; universities provided them with researchers; governments built systems of transportation and communication—governments even fostered markets at home and protected them abroad. The ideology of free enterprise was now gradually replaced by a philosophy—Pope John Paul II calls it "neo-liberal"—that was more socially oriented. It recognized that social peace was essential for the success of a business civilization, and for this reason supported welfare measures to remove the glaring injustices from society. In the United States, this neo-capitalism arrived with President Roosevelt's New Deal; in Canada after the Second World War. In this second phase, capitalism was no longer "rigid"; it was softened to a certain degree. An increase of wealth took place among a wide section of the population, including the workers. Exploitation and insecurity remained also in this phase, but thanks to the pressure of organized labour and the people, Western societies experienced conditions of prosperity that were previously unknown.

This somewhat more benign phase of capitalism, John Paul II argues, has come to an end. We now enter upon a third phase, created by the internationalization of capital and the new computer-based technology. Other historical factors contribute to the present crisis, in particular the emergence on the political scene of peoples or nations that had previously been subjugated. Then there is the rising cost of energy and raw materials. In order to reorganize the creation of capital, the new giant corporations now shed their link to the nation in which their head office is located, they drop the neo-liberal philosophy, and they withdraw from the social consensus of the New Deal. They reconstitute capital and production on an international scale to protect and promote their own economic interests alone. They appeal to an ideology that again makes freedom and free enterprise the key phrases, while in fact the corporations are just about the only free agents left in society.

At the same time, our generation has discovered that natural resources are limited, that water and air are threatened by pollution and that the earth surface is vulnerable. While these discoveries would demand new policies, slowing down industrial growth and protecting the environment, the corporations involved in reorganizing their capital remain indifferent to these problems. Because ever-larger sectors of the population are being excluded from economic well-being and pushed into poverty, the corporations increasingly rely on governments to pacify the population and protect their empires. What they view as needed is new stress on law and order, new legislation to restrict the power of workers, massive propaganda that makes criticism of capitalism appear unpatriotic, and an individualistic ideology that makes the successful focus on their own lives and close their eyes to the existing injustices. Because the United States makes the world safe for world capitalism, the U.S. government, usually backed by the Canadian government, has been willing to defend military juntas in Third World countries, despite the most cruel violation of human rights. A critical report on Canada's nuclear arms policy, produced by the Canadian churches (December 1982), says:

> Nuclear weapons are becoming part of the means by which Northern industrial states compete for influence and domination in the Third World and

> by which they seek to keep a place in a world economic order that bestows extraordinary benefits on the powerful and that exacts extraordinary costs from the powerless.[22]

According to Pope John Paul II:

> It is not for the Church to analyse scientifically the consequences these changes may have on human society. But the Church considers it to be its task to call attention to the dignity and the rights of those who work, to condemn situations in which that dignity and those rights are violated, and to help to guide the above-mentioned changes so as to ensure authentic progress by man and society. (*Laborem Exercens*, n. 1)

The New Year's Statement, read in conjunction with *Laborem Exercens*, sees the capitalist system at the present time as moving into a new phase, characterized by greater brutality than ever before. Millions of people in the less developed parts of the world are threatened to be forever pushed outside of the economic system. These enlarged forms of injustice on the world scale, John Paul II thinks, are "much more extensive than those which in the last century" oppressed workers (n. 8). As the reaction to the early phase of capitalism was "a great burst of solidarity between workers," "a reaction important and eloquent from the viewpoint of social ethics," so, the Pope hopes, the reaction of workers and the marginalized to the present crisis will give rise to a new burst of solidarity to found movements of resistance. "In order to achieve social justice in the various parts of the world, in the various countries and in the relationship between them, there is a need for ever new movements of solidarity of workers and with the workers" (n. 8).

The Statement's Religious and Cultural Meanings

Before turning to the proposals made by the bishops, it is important to examine the religious meaning and the cultural impact of their statement. The religious foundation of the "option for the poor" has already been mentioned. While this commentary is not the place to engage in an extended theological reflection on the New Year's Statement, it is necessary to say at least a few words about its religious implications.

The emergence in the Church of a new social theory, beginning in Latin America and making its way to Europe and North America, is based on new religious experiences. Before the option for the poor was spelled out in ecclesiastical documents, it was embodied in the spiritual stance of small Christian communities struggling for justice.[23] These Christian communities were confirmed in their action by reading the Scriptures, by praying together and by celebrating the Eucharist. They experienced the God of the Bible as on their side. They heard God's Word speaking to them through the experience of Israel as recorded in the Old Testament and through the experience of Jesus as recorded in the New. For them the promises of Christ included the liberation of the oppressed. In their experience, Christian faith and commitment to justice were welded together.

This new religious experience, expressed in prayers, public worship, song and poetry, was communicated to Catholics in other parts of the world. This experience became available to Christians who were not among the oppressed but who had committed themselves to justice on their behalf. What Pope John Paul II called "solidarity of the poor and with the poor" was not simply a political commitment, a secular stance; it was, properly speaking, a religious conversion in which resounded the whole of the Gospel. This conversion gave rise to a religious yearning for justice. Thanks to this passionate yearning, "the others," especially the oppressed others, became part of one's own personal consciousness. "The others" could no longer be excluded from one's own self-definition; "the others" began to make up the abiding backdrop against which one's private, day-to-day experiences took on their true meaning.

According to traditional Catholic teaching, Christian faith becomes fully alive only when it is carried by hope and love. Theologians spoke of *fides charitate formata* ("faith given shape by love"). Thanks to the new religious experience and the support it received from the Scriptures, Christian faith is now seen to be fully alive only when it is carried by hope, love and, above all, justice. It is possible to speak of *fides justitia formata* ("faith given shape by justice"). Why is this so? Because in a society in which injustice is structurally imposed, love transforms itself into a yearning for justice and into action to transform the status quo. In this perspective, faith includes the commitment to justice. The option for the poor, then, is a dimension of Christian faith. That is why the Puebla Conference (n. 1134) said that the option for the poor will eventually lead to "the conversion" of the entire Church. And that is why the Canadian bishops said, in their 1976 Labour Day Statement (n. 7), that the minority of Catholics who follow the social gospel are a public sign summoning the entire Church to greater fidelity.

The reason why it is important to spell out the religious foundation of the Church's shift to the left is that many of its vehement critics have charged that this recent development is a purely secular movement, one that leads to the decline of religious faith. In an interview on a Canadian television network, Peter Berger, the well-known American sociologist who defends the neo-conservative cause in the United States, argued that the preoccupation with social justice leads to the secularization of the Church and hence to the weakening of its religious mission. He argued that priests, theologians and leading lay people have lost confidence in the Christian message and find religion uninteresting. They have now turned to the political order to find there a substitute religion. Yet the historical evidence does not support Berger's hypothesis. The testimonies of Third World Christians whose faith includes commitment to liberation are well recorded.[24] Some of them, including Archbishop Oscar Romero of El Salvador, have become martyrs. Even in the developed countries, testimonies abound that faith in Jesus Christ has come to include a commitment to justice, an option for the poor.

These new religious experiences are confirmed by a theological development in the Church that deserves attention. In the past, the Catholic Church tended to define the Church's mission as the proclamation of the Gospel so that the world may believe. The Church at that time also recognized a secondary mission, subordinate to the first, defined in terms of social justice. While the Church's primary mission was spiritual, supernatural, and related to the order of salvation, the secondary mission, guided by Catholic social teaching, was earthly, natural, and related to secular society. The two missions remained distinct. What has happened at the Vatican Council (1962-65), and more especially since the early Seventies, is that under the impact of the new religious experience of faith-and-justice, the Catholic Church has begun to define its mission in terms that include both salvation and earthly liberation. Beginning with the 1971 Synod of Bishops, to which mention has already been given, the Church has recognized that the proclamation of the Gospel includes an active witness to social justice and human rights. According to the same synod, the redemption Jesus Christ has brought includes the liberation of peoples from oppression. There is then a single mission of the Church, uniting faith and justice, which proclaims the gospel message of new life and supports the struggle against domination.

The theology of the Church's single mission was endorsed in Pope John Paul II's first encyclical, *Redemptor Hominis*, which claims that Jesus Christ has identified himself with every human being and all of humanity and that, for this reason, the Church's defence of human rights and its commitment to social justice are therefore a service rendered to Jesus Christ and to society in his name.[25] In this encyclical, Jesus appears as the protector of humans and the liberator of the oppressed. The two orders, the natural and the supernatural, are seen to cohere in a single history. God appears here as the transcendent mystery, operative in history, the matrix of human well-being, and the underlying thrust of people's struggle for peace and emancipation.

At this point it is worth mentioning that the Catholic bishops' statement received strong support from the leaders of the major Christian churches. Ted Scott, primate of the Anglican Church in Canada, Clark MacDonald, moderator of the United Church of Canada, and Wayne Smith, moderator of the Presbyterian Church, made public declarations in the press to express their solidarity with the Catholic bishops. Reverend Wayne Smith had this to say:

> Presbyterians should find no difficulty in identifying with the principles that underlie the Catholic bishops' statement. It is a logical expression of our historical concern for civil and religious liberties, and the economic rights of the disadvantaged in our society. Further, the bishops concern for the value and dignity of work has its parallel in the Reformed emphasis that people are accountable to God for the use of Creation.... We are directed by Christ to listen to the voices of the poor and the powerless in our midst. We as Christians are called to struggle for economic justice and participate in building a new society.... It is impossible for those who stand within the tradition of Jean Calvin and John Knox to remain silent on the social and economic issues that touch the lives of God's people at such a profound level. I pray that my fellow Presbyterians will join me in responding positively to the bishops' invitation for a pilgrimage together.[26]

This strong support of the Canadian churches is

no coincidence. Since the early Seventies, the Canadian churches have been in dialogue on many issues of social justice, have collaborated in the setting up of interchurch committees to act in this field, and have produced joint statements on economic and social problems for submission to the federal cabinet and to royal commissions. There has come about a certain ecumenical consensus among church leaders, a consensus that is not always shared by church members in the pew. A similar approach to social justice issues has been worked out in the Canadian Council of Churches and, on the international level, in the World Council of Churches, with its head office in Geneva, Switzerland. On the level of its leadership, the Christian church has shifted its loyalty to the sector of human society that is made up by the disadvantaged, the poor and the oppressed.

The New Year's Statement also has a cultural impact that deserves attention. Canadians reacted strongly to the statement. Opinions were sharply divided. There were the strong voices of government representatives, political leaders, business executives and editorial writers who found the statement inappropriate, misguided, naive, badly informed, idealistic or even ideological. A few denied the right of the bishops to speak on matters affecting the economy. There were also strong voices, speaking from a different social location, that supported the bishops' statement and recommended it as the basis for a nation-wide debate. Among these favourable voices were the leaders of the other Canadian churches, representatives of labour organizations, national and local, leaders of the New Democratic Party, a few elected members of the traditional parties whose social concern was well known, and spokespersons for city councils and other organizations concerned with city life. Among the supporting voices were some newspaper columnists, social critics and left-leaning economists. Support for the statement also came from vast numbers of people who were suffering from the present recession, especially the unemployed and workers with job insecurity. The support given to the statement did not mean that people necessarily agreed with all of its recommendations: it simply meant that they approved the statement as a good analysis of the ills of society and as a basis for a debate on what is to be done to remedy the moral disorder in this country. Examining the reactions to the New Year's Statement should allow one to draw a line through Canadian society revealing the contours of an existing class conflict. This topic will be taken up later in this chapter.

The first cultural effect of the statement is that it "de-sacralizes" the present order. Mainstream culture tends to present the status quo as normative. It makes people think that even the unhappy aspects of their social existence are "natural" or "normal." No use getting excited about them: they are part of life. In theological language, every society is regarded as sinful, and it is the ambiguous task of mainstream culture to make this sin invisible. Since the contradictions of society become a source of restlessness and instability, society seems to be in need of an ideology, a set of ideas and symbols, that legitimates the existing order, disguises the contradictions, makes the injustices appear minor and suggests that the way things are is normal. What takes place here is a certain "sacralization" of the present order. People begin to feel that it is disloyal to doubt the values and institutions approved by society. They learn not to ask certain questions. Even when the present order makes them suffer—for instance, through unemployment, job insecurity and destitution—they shy away from challenging the existing economic system. Public ideology is so powerful that people easily put the blame on innocent groups, or they accuse themselves for being failures and feel guilty.

In the Canadian context the New Year's Statement de-sacralized the present order. It allowed people to distance themselves from the public ideology and take a critical look at the socio-economic realty as it is. "There is nothing 'natural' or 'normal' about present unemployment rates," the statement says (s. 5). In several public addresses Bishop Remi de Roo, the president of the Social Affairs Commission of the Canadian Conference of Catholic Bishops, criticized the idea of "normalcy" that mainstream culture tries to promote. According to Father Bill Ryan, the provincial of the English-speaking Jesuits in Canada, himself an economist, the statement reveals that "the emperor has no clothes on." The inherited system that we were taught to admire and defend simply does not deliver the goods. Despite the assurances of the government, and the political leaders and economists associated with it, the system does not work well. Our "normal" wisdom turns out to be very unwise.

A second cultural effect of the New Year's Statement is that a certain language critical of capitalism is made legitimate, a language that was previously "taboo" in Canadian society. The bishops recognize that the present recession is "symptomatic of a much larger structural crisis in the international system of capitalism" (s. 2). They use a vocabulary and propose ideas that are often labelled as socialist, "red" or "Marxist" and dismissed without a hearing. They contrast the interests of the poor and the rich, of workers and owners, of the marginal and the powerful. They point to the conflictual nature of Canadian society, where government and industries pursue policies that place the burden of the economic decline unevenly on the shoulders of ordinary people. The bishops repeatedly stress the need for "alternative models of economic development," recommending worker and community ownership of the industries. They ask that labour unions be allowed to participate in the decisions affecting production and economic policy. They insist on the priority of labour over capital.

Some members of Parliament have complained that the bishops' statement is inspired by "Marxist" ideas. They are quite mistaken. What has taken place is the emergence of a new Catholic social theory, first in Latin America and then in the World Church, which has developed its own critique of capitalism on the basis of biblical prophecy, the experiences of oppressed peoples, and traditional Catholic social teaching. This new Catholic social theory has been worked out through critical dialogue with Marxist ideas, but it has created its own independent orientation and its own original vocabulary. Its foundation is theological. Its principal bias is that the God of the Bible is partial—that

God stands on the side of the poor and oppressed against the empires of this world. It is of great cultural importance for countries like Canada to have access to a language critical of the existing order that is grounded in the Christian tradition.

A Christian critique of capitalist society is not a new Canadian phenomenon. The Protestant social gospel from the end of the nineteenth century right into the Thirties provided a critical tradition, derived from biblical faith, that made an important contribution to the evolution of Canadian society. In particular, it was one of the significant forces in the movement that created the Co-operative Commonwealth Federation (CCF) in the early Thirties.[27]

Finally, the New Year's Statement invites Canadians to imagine an alternative society. The bishops repeatedly speak of "alternative models of economic development" and "alternative economic vision and policies." While the imagination of people tends to be limited to what is possible within the boundaries defined by the dominant culture, and hence imagination often remains a prisoner of the present, the New Year's Statement bursts this framework and introduces the image of a more just society, at odds with the structures and policies that form the present one. What the bishops speak of is no political never-never land, no happy fiction nor idealist vision; it is rather a utopia, a vision of an alternative society, close enough to the as yet unexplored potentialities of the present to generate imaginative, but workable social and political strategies. What guides the new Catholic social theory is not an idealized image of medieval society (this was true for corporatism), not an image of the present society, fine tuned and adjusted, but the image of a future society hidden in the possibilities of the present yet qualitatively different from it. It is in this sense that the New Year's Statement appeals to utopia.

Social scientists have come to speak of the political meaning of culture. They argue that the present economic and political order is kept in place not so much by the power of the state, threatening the use of force, but by the cultural mainstream, by the ideas, symbols, values and priorities, mediated by newspapers, radio and television, by the schools, by the taken-for-granted wisdom expressed in daily conversation, by what passes as common sense, by the standard approach to the education of children, and so forth. Mainstream culture makes alternatives to the present appear as extreme, "far out," idealistic, irresponsible, naive or, at best, ahead of their time. In this sense does the dominant culture exert political power. If a movement for significant social change is to be successful, it must be accompanied by a cultural strategy that invites people to think new thoughts and experience the attraction of an alternative vision. While religion is usually a conservative force protecting the present order, there have always been times when religion was prophetic and utopian, when it released people from the present and instilled a yearning in them for a more just, an alternative, society.[28] The New Year's Statement, summing up the recent Catholic social teaching, is an expression of such prophetic religion. It invites Canadians to engage in alternative thinking.

The cultural impact of the New Year's Statement includes a rejection of positivistic science. Against the economists who regard economics as a value-free science, the bishops insist that economics and ethics are interrelated. Some critics have objected to the statement, claiming that ethics has nothing to do with economics. In many cases, these remarks are part of a polemic against the statement and are not intended to be taken literally. For it seems almost obvious that if you remove ethics from economic activity, such activity would degenerate very quickly: like any large-scale human enterprise, it depends on loyalties, cooperation, trust, reliability, honesty and so forth. The separation of ethics from the social and economic project would spell the end of civilization.

Implicit in every approach to economics is a concept of human nature. If economists seriously wish to defend the value-free nature of their science, they have to assume that human beings act in a predictable fashion, always doing what is economically most advantageous for them. Human behaviour, they have to assume, is determined by the laws of economics. While such an approach may produce some useful research for the production and marketing of goods and even at times come up with policies that enable government or corporations to achieve the result they desire, still it is based on a truncated concept of human nature and hence cannot lay claim to universality. Research in the field of economics is always guided by a particular social philosophy. Duncan Cameron will deal with this question at greater length in the following chapter. Suffice it to say that in Canada there are several research institutes, each conducting economic research, each using the scientific method, but each coming to different conclusions. Why?

Because these institutes operate out of different theoretical presuppositions. On the right, there is the Fraser Institute, following a free-enterprise philosphy; then there is the C. D. Howe Institute, the Conference Board of Canada and the Canadian Institute for Economic Policy in the middle ground; and on the left, the Canadian Centre for Policy Alternatives, following a social democratic perspective. The scientific method does not lead to agreement in economics.

The Proposals

We now turn to the proposals made by the Canadian bishops. Duncan Cameron's commentary will discuss them in detail from an economist's point of view. In this commentary, we simply wish to point to their dialogical form, explain that they can be read in both a reformist and a more radical way, and show that throughout the bishops remain non-partisan; that is, they cannot be identified with any political party or labour organization in Canada.

There are two sets of proposals, one to be put into practice immediately, the other pointing in the direction of a long-range transformation. Both sets of proposals, the statement argues, are based on the fundamental principles, "the option for the poor" and "the priority of labour over capital."

The short-range proposals are the following:

- we must recognize unemployment rather than inflation as the number one problem to overcome;
- we need an industrial strategy to create jobs;
- we must shift the burden of the economic decline to the earners of higher income;

- we must stop the cutbacks of welfare and social services; and
- we must ask labour unions to participate in the making of industrial policies.

While these proposals are similar to those made by the Canadian labour movement, they retain their non-partisan character. In particular, they offer critical remarks in regard to labour organizations. They ask that labour unions seek greater cooperation with unorganized labour and with the unemployed. They admit that "limited perspectives and excessive demands" are sometimes also connected with labour organizations. These short-range proposals could be understood simply as the rejection of the monetary economic policies, or "Reaganomics," adopted by the Canadian government, and as an urgent plea to return to the Keynesian economic policies that since the Second World War have guided Western capitalist countries into prosperity.

What are the long-term proposals made in the New Year's Statement? They are formulated as an invitation to a nation-wide debate. Instead of offering guidelines, the bishops outline the terms of a public discussion. How do they do this? They first describe the present trends of the economy, which they regard as misguided; then they describe countertrends that move in the opposite direction; and finally they ask people to debate among themselves how far the shift of emphasis to the countertrends should go. Many commentators have overlooked the dialogical form in which the bishops have made their proposals. These commentators thought that the bishops ask Canadians to stand wholly behind the countertrends, while they actually only ask for a shift of emphasis and want Canadians to debate how far this shift of emphasis should go.

What are these trends and countertrends? First, there is the present trend towards the multiplication of megaprojects that rely on the export of natural resources and employ relatively few workers. The countertrend is here the development of the manufacturing sector so that manufactured goods are produced in Canada for the use of Canadians. How far should the shift of emphasis go?

A second trend of the present economy is the conversion of the industries to high technology without plans for employing the workers who lose their jobs. The countertrend to this is the protection of the labour-intensive industries in Canada and the search for an "appropriate technology," one that takes into account the need for jobs. How far will the shift in the new direction go? Some critics have suggested that the bishops are against computer technology altogether. This is not so. What the bishops oppose is the conversion to high technology that is not accompanied by strategies for future employment. The decision to introduce high technology must not simply be based on the quest for higher profit margins; it must include concern for employment.

A third trend of the present economy is the concentration of capital. Corporations become larger and larger; they increase their power. The economic decisions that affect the lives of Canadians are passing into the hands of an ever-shrinking elite, often people who do not even live in Canada. The countertrend is here the decentralization of capital, first by promoting local industries, especially in the less developed parts of Canada, and secondly by introducing new forms of ownership, in particular worker and community ownership. How far shall we move in this direction?

A fourth trend of the present economy, related to the previous one, is the growing foreign ownership of Canadian industries. The countertrend is the promotion of a self-reliant economy. The word "self-reliant" is taken from Latin American ecclesiastical documents that protest against the dependency of national economies and demand "self-reliant development" as the economic road towards the people's liberation. How far shall Canadian society move in this direction?

A fifth trend of the present economy is the granting of tax privileges to the large corporations in the hope that high profits will make them reinvest their wealth in new industrial developments and thus create jobs. What guarantees do we have that the corporations will do this? They are more likely, the bishops think, to reinvest their capital in labour-saving technology, move it to another country or spend it on market speculation or luxury goods. The countertrend is an industrial strategy that does not expect the private sector to be the engine that moves Canada into economic recovery—instead it assumes responsibility for economic planning. How far shall we move in this direction?

Together these proposals call for "alternative models of economic development." Needed in Canadian society are "alternative economic vision and strategies." Despite their boldness, these proposals, because of their dialogical form, can be read in a reformist and in a more radical way. In my opinion, they cannot simply be understood as a call to return to the Keynesian economy of the past. In particular the demand for the decentralization of capital has more far-reaching implications. Even if the statement is read as recommending simply the reform of capitalism, it is a "system-transcending reform," in the sense defined earlier, that is being proposed. For here the principle of reform transcends the existing system and hence promises in the long run to transform the system in a qualitative way and thus move beyond it. Yet the proposals also allow for a more radical reading, recommending models of economic development at odds with capitalist ideas. The tension between reformist ideas and more radical proposals is part of the public debate initiated by the Canadian bishops.

At the same time, the New Year's Statement is non-partisan in the sense that it does not speak out of an identification with any existing political party or labour organization. The bishops claim that "as pastors their concern about the economy is not based on any specific political options" (s. 1). In particular, the statement does not endorse the NDP nor the Canadian Labour Congress. On the contrary, it challenges all political organizations, including these latter. It can be argued that the statement offers a more radical critique of society than does the NDP, in particular by recommending the decentralization of capital and the cooperation of labour unions in the making of economic policy. As most social democratic parties, the NDP stands in a centralist tradition; it easily gives the impression that its ideal is an economy planned by a democratically controlled central administration. It is only now beginning to think of Canadian society in more decentralizing terms. The bishops' statement challenges the NDP to recover the commitment of the CCF to cooperative ownership and other alternative models of economic development. Because the CLC is wary in regard to workers' participation, fearing the co-option of labour by the capitalists, the NDP has left undeveloped its own, older heritage. Much of the language of economic reform adopted by the NDP sounds Keynesian and could just as well come from the traditional parties. The "old left" in the NDP, the so-called left caucus, more critical of the existing order and more socialist in its ideas, still trusts the old remedy of massive nationalization, even though historical experience has shown that state ownership is no guarantee that industrial and economic institutions will be run for the benefit of the people. Catholic social thought, since Pope Pius XI, has approved of nationalization whenever private ownership puts power into the hands of the few so as to prevent government from protecting the common good.[29] Still, the thrust of Catholic social teaching is towards the decentralization of ownership. The Canadian bishops, it has been noted, while putting great stress on a rational industrial policy and hence on responsible economic planning, do not say a word about nationalization. According to the Catholic ideal, the centralizing trend of overall economic planning should be counterbalanced by the decentralizing trend of ownership, in particular through community and worker ownership of the industries.

Nor is the statement written out of an identification with the CLC. While the Canadian bishops, in keeping with the teaching of Pope John Paul II, regard the labour movement as the dynamic element of modern society, they also raise critical questions in regard to the existing labour organizations. In particular, they urge the labour organizations to manifest more clearly their solidarity with the unorganized workers and the unemployed. Labour organizations that simply aim at improving the economic conditions of their members have become unfaithful to the historical vocation of the labour movement, which is to protest against injustice and be the social agent for the transformation of society. Narrowness of view, the bishops say, is something that also affects labour unions. What the bishops have in mind, and here again they follow Pope John Paul II, is the creation of a movement of solidarity in Canada, built around the labour struggles for justice and embracing all the victims of society, in particular the unemployed and those who for various reasons have been marginalized (the Native Peoples, certain immigrant groups, the neglected aged, and so forth). Labour is to be the main actor in this social movement.

Meeting in May, 1983, the Social Affairs Commission of the Canadian Conference of Catholic Bishops reconfirmed the orientation of their January statement. In a press release, they mentioned in particular that their role is not to become directly involved in partisan politics. Instead, they believe that what is required today is "the building of an independent popular or social movement for economic justice that embraces working and non-working people in solidarity, brings together local grassroots groups, forms coalitions, and eventually becomes a force to be reckoned with in Canadian society."

The Church as Prophet

The following sections will examine some of the objections made against the statement on theological grounds by Christians. Not all objections are of a serious nature. Some are based on a careless reading of the text. Several critics of the statement, for instance, have complained that the bishops are against profit, that profit is a dirty word for them, that they envisage an economy where profit plays no part. But this is mistaken. Everyone knows that an industry or a business must pay for itself and make some profit. What the statement has criticized is the "maximization of profit," that is, decisions regarding production and resources that give priority to the search for ever-greater profit over other factors, especially those affecting the well-being of workers. There are, however, many objections that raise serious questions and deserve careful attention.

The first one is the accusation that what is taking place in the Catholic Church at this time, and in the Canadian Catholic Church in particular, is "a clericalism of the left." In the past Catholic bishops interfered in the political life of their country—in Europe in particular, but also in Quebec—and violated the appropriate responsibility of the laity; now, after a few decades of non-interference, bishops again intervene in the temporal order, albeit this time on the left. Members of the Liberal party, especially French Canadians who remember the old days of right-wing clericalism, have protested against the New Year's Statement as a new manifestation of clericalism. To bolster their position, these politicians, including Marc Lalonde, referred to Jacques Maritain, the influential Catholic social philosopher prior to Vatican Council II (1962-65). It is important, they say, to distinguish between the sacred and the profane (temporal) order. The power of bishops in the Church has to do with the sphere of the sacred. It is there, in the field of doctrine, liturgy and church organization, that Catholics owe them obedience. But the profane or temporal is the proper sphere of the laity. Enlightened by the moral principles taught by pope and bishops, Christian lay people exercise their responsibility in society in complete freedom, without interference from the Church hierarchy. They, the laity, are the agents of the Gospel in matters affecting the social and political order. The Canadian bishops, they argue, have transgressed their authority.

Since in the past Catholic bishops, including the popes, have exercised vast political power, violated the freedom of the laity, and often protected the most reactionary forces in society, the objection must be taken seriously. The clear distinction between the two realms, the sacred and the secular introduced into Catholic social teaching by Pope Leo XIII, was the result of an historical development in the direction of freedom and moral maturity. Jacques Maritain and other social thinkers rendered an important service to the Church when they insisted on the independent Christian responsibility of the laity against the old custom of clerical control. Yet even these thinkers admitted that when it was a matter of condemning sin (*ratione peccati*) bishops had the right and duty to make their voices heard in society. Since the Canadian bishops identify present unemployment and its human consequences as a moral disorder or social sin, their statement—even from this pre-Vatican II perspective—does not violate the principles that protect the freedom of the laity.

Of much greater importance, however, is the evolution of the Church's social teaching during and after Vatican Council II. Both theoretically and practically the Catholic Church has modified the perception of its mission and the role it must play in society. The Church has become "a different ball game." In particular, as mentioned several times above, the strict separation of the two orders of the sacred and the profane (the supernatural and the natural) has been overcome through the recognition that divine grace is operative not only in the Christian community but in the whole of human history. The two orders, though distinct, cohere in a single history. "That the earthly and the heavenly city penetrate each other is a fact accessible to faith," said Vatican Council II (*Gaudium et Spes*, n. 40). God is the transcendent mystery operative in people's historical struggles to create a human, just and pacified world. It is for this reason that the Church's mission has come to be defined in a new way: included in the proclamation of the Christian Gospel is the affirmation of human rights and social justice as well as action on behalf of the people whose rights and whose justice are being violated. While in the past the Church's social teaching played a subordinate role in the exercise of its mission, today it has moved into the centre of attention because social justice is conceived as part and parcel of the message of Jesus Christ. We have here the emergence of the Church as critic of society, as prophet denouncing the violations of justice, as preacher summoning the believing community to responsible action. All Christians are called to give witness in this way; but those who speak for the Church as a whole, the bishops, have a special duty to speak up for social justice.

This is not the place to analyze the historical development that has produced this new sense of mission during and after the Vatican Council. One important historical factor was the Church's repentance over the silence it observed during the years of European fascism, in particular during the Nazi period with its violation of human rights and its genocidal projects.

To gain a better understanding of the Church's role in society, it is valuable to analyze the several ways in which the Church exercises political influence. The first one is as "legitimator of the inherited order." Here the Church sees itself as the guardian of a Christian culture, which it tries to defend against the influence of secularism, pluralism and individualism. This is how the Church has acted in the Catholic countries of Europe after the advent of Enlightenment and modernization. The attempt to protect the inherited culture often made the Church the ally of conservative and even reactionary forces in society. Catholic social teaching in this context gave this legitimating function a certain reformist thrust. In Quebec, too, the Church acted as the protector of a Catholic order against the influx of Protestant and secular modernity. Secondly, the Church may act politically as "lobby for its own interests." This is how the Church acted when it held a minority position in a neutral or hostile climate. In English-speaking countries, where Catholics were in a minority and often socially despised, the political activity of the Church was confined to efforts to protect its freedom, to defend the rights of its people and to support various Catholic institutions deemed necessary for the growth and well-being of the Catholic community. Only in a more remote sense was the Church in such situations also the defender of the existing order. In English-speaking countries, Catholics, largely members of the working class, supported the reform parties, the Labour party in England and, for several historical reasons, the Liberal party in Canada.

In some countries, under special historical circumstances, both the first and the second model gave rise to Catholic political parties: there have been Catholic parties that wanted to protect the inherited Catholic culture, and there have been others that protected the Church in a situation of disadvantage.

A third way of exercising political influence occurs in situations of national oppression, such as in Poland and Ireland where the Catholic Church became a "symbol of identity and resistance" and as such acquired considerable power in the consciousness of the people. Here the Church gained great political authority.

There is, however, a fourth way, a more theological one, in which the Church exercises political influence in society. The Church may become "the promoter of gospel values." Here the Church, relying on the biblical call for justice, becomes the critic of society. Here it exercises a prophetic function, transcending its immediate institutional self-interest and entering into solidarity with the whole of society, especially the poor and defenceless. This is the role the Church now perceives for itself, as it was defined at Vatican Council II and intensified by the Church's subsequent historical experience. In this sense, the Church has become "a new ball game." In the name of gospel values (the option for the poor, and the dignity of labour), the Canadian bishops have become critics of society. In the name of gospel values (the dignity of human life), the American bishops have condemned the nuclear arms race and demanded a nuclear freeze. For the Church, this is politics in a new mode.

At one time, accusations of clericalism were raised by lay people who opposed the Church's identification with the conservative sector of society or who felt that the Church was excessively concerned with the survival of its own institutions. Lay people wanted to promote political action more in line with the ideals of Catholic social theory. Here independence from the hierarchy was necessary. This principle still holds today whenever bishops make political decisions based on the old ways, abstracting from theological principles, to defend the status quo or to protect their institutional interests. However, whenever the Church understands itself as a prophet and as promoter of gospel values, then the bishops have a special duty to speak out and exercise political leadership. The call to give witness to Christian values applies, of course, to all Christians, but the bishops alone are able to speak in the name of the entire Catholic community and its biblical faith. Because they speak in the name of many, their word has more authority. Since they speak on behalf of the people at the base and in the margin, people whose voice is weak and in some cases not heard at all, the bishops become the spokesmen for the oppressed part of the laity. This is not clericalism. In the countries of Latin America, moreover, the bishops have greater security in giving witness to the demands of justice. They cannot lose their jobs; they have no wife and children who can be made to suffer for them. And when they are imprisoned or assassinated, they have as martyrs a special power in the Catholic community.

Even in Canada the public reaction to the New Year's Statement has shown that the contrast between hierarchy and laity is no longer a useful principle explaining the behaviour and attitudes of Catholics. When the bishops of the Social Affairs Commission opted for the workers, the unemployed and low-income people, the reaction of the laity was greatly divided. Even a casual look at the responses reveals that Canadians (including Catholics) who were suffering from the economic crisis or were in solidarity with those who were, welcomed the statement with enthusiasm. Only the laity who defended the status quo raised the objection of clericalism.

Once the public declarations of the Church opt for the people at the base and in the margin, a certain conflict in the Catholic community is unavoidable. The conflict reaches right into the community of bishops. Cardinal Emmet Carter, Archbishop of Toronto, called a press conference on the day after the statement was released in order to disassociate himself from its message. While many Christian and secular organizations in the country organized meetings to promote the Church's social teaching, Cardinal Carter fostered a wait-and-see approach by organizing public hearings in which groups and persons in Toronto were able to express their opinions for and against the statement. The option for the people at the base and in the margin draws a dividing line right through the Church, with hierarchy and laity on both sides. In this context, the old issue of clericalism has lost its meaning.

At the same time, the Church's new social teaching does not violate the consciences of Catholics. In order to clarify to what extent Catholics are bound in conscience, it may be useful to distinguish among "universal moral principles," "middle-range positions," and the "practical applications." Middle-range positions concretize what universal moral principles mean in the actual conditions of history. When it comes to universal principles, Catholics will be inclined to follow the Church's teaching. Most of them will think that this is what they must do. When it comes to middle-range positions, Catholics are not bound in the same way. Here they are urged to listen carefully to the Church's position, re-examine their own opinion, return to the moral foundations in the Scriptures, and come to a new, more carefully argued position. Here it is possible to differ responsibly from the bishops' teachings. In their prophetic teachings, neither bishops nor pope have suggested that they want to bind the critical conscience of Catholics. In the area of practical application, furthermore, bishops have nothing to say, unless such applications violate a moral norm.

It is possible to argue that "the option for the poor" and "the value and dignity of labour" are universal moral principles derived from Scripture. What these principles mean in the concrete historical order is brought out by middle-range positions, for instance, the decentralization of capital and the cooperative ownership of industry. The concentration of capital in private hands is here seen as excluding workers and the great majority of people from responsible participation in society. Catholics who after new reflection decide not to follow this teaching must provide new arguments, at least to themselves, showing that in the present situation workers and the great majority of people are in fact not dominated. When it comes to practical applications—for instance, how to decentralize capital in Canada—the bishops are silent. They would regard giving directions in the practical order as exceeding their responsibility.

Beyond the Welfare State

A second important objection to the New Year's Statement concerns the call for full employment and the emphasis on the dignity of labour. This involves several issues. On the practical level the critics wonder whether it is wise and realistic to ask for full employment at this time. Do we want an endless increase in the production of goods? Do we not get ecological signals that the time has come to slow down industrial growth? And further, with the advent of computer technology, must we not expect that industrial production in the future will use fewer workers, and thus resign ourselves to the fact that vast numbers of workers will never find work again? In such a situation, is it not more realistic to ask for a guaranteed annual income so that people can survive with some dignity, even if there are no jobs for them? How can one justify the demand of full employment at this time?

On the pastoral level, the critics raise equally important issues. Is it wise, they ask, to put emphasis on the dignity of labour and to derive the meaning of human existence from work? Since a multitude of people are without jobs, should the Church not help them to acquire a spirituality that affirms their dignity even though they are unemployed? Does not the emphasis on the dignity of labour drive people without jobs deeper into despair? Should we not insist that human dignity resides in a person's spiritual nature and hence is quite independent of the work he or she does? More than that, does not the emphasis on the dignity of labour introduce into Catholicism the so-called Protestant ethic, or work ethic, that directs people's energies to doing and making, neglects the contemplative dimension of life, and thus robs them of leisure, poetry and play?

Before we reply to these difficulties, we note that the Canadian bishops are following the special direction of Pope John Paul II's *Laborem Exercens*. While the encyclical recognizes the changed conditions created by the new technology, and in fact speaks of a second industrial revolution, it nonetheless calls for full employment. It regards unemployment as a dreadful plague from which society must be delivered. The same encyclical also puts an emphasis on the dignity of labour that is new in Catholic social teaching. A sentence that has puzzled many readers says this: "Man's life is built up every day from work, from work it derives its special dignity" (n. 1). In a speech given by John Paul II to the International Labour Conference (June 1980), we find a similar statement: "In work is revealed the meaning of man's existence." This is startling. According to the more traditional teaching, the dignity of work was derived from man's spiritual nature. Work, even lowly service, was of great dignity because it was human work, because it was performed by a spiritual person. For Pope John Paul, in contrast, it is from work that the special dignity of man is derived.

The Canadian bishops hint at this teaching when they say: "It is through the activity of work that people are able to exercise their creative spirit, realize their human dignity, and share in Creation" (s. 1).

While this commentary is not the place to discuss the philosophical and theological background from which John Paul II derives his position, we have to take some notice of it. *Laborem Exercens* defines the human being as worker.[30] Man differs from the animals because man alone works. Through labour, human beings create the conditions of their survival and well-being, and in doing so, they also realize themselves, they also create their consciousness, they also affirm themselves as subjects, that is, as responsible artisans and authors of their world. Needless to say, John Paul II does not link this theory of man's self-constitution through labour to a materialistic ontology! For the Pope, God as Creator and Redeemer is present in the process by which people constitute their world and thereby enter into inwardness, responsibility, dignity and subjectivity. According to the Pope, the subjective dimension of work—that is, man's self-realization—has precedence over the objective dimension of labour, which is the world humans create. This is his peculiarly Christian emphasis. What counts most in man's labouring is the spiritual dimension, people becoming ever more "subject," people fulfilling their vocation, people assuming responsibility for one another and their world, people being creators in the image of God the Creator. In this sense, then, it is from labour that human dignity is derived and in labouring that the meaning of man's existence is revealed.

This process, the encyclical says, is universal.

> It embraces all human beings, every generation, every phase of economic and cultural development, and at the same time is a process that takes place within each human being, in each conscious human subject. Each and every human being is at the same time embraced by it. Each and every individual, to the proper extent and in an incalculable number of ways, takes part in the giant process whereby man "subdues the earth" through labour. (n. 4)

What follows from this is that labour cannot simply be identified with jobs, for every service offered to society, on any level whatever, if it is truly a service, deserves the name of labour. At the same time, labour cannot simply be separated from jobs because the labour to which people are called must be regular, sustained, coordinated and the title for their access to society's wealth. While the welfare state is an urgent necessity in the present order, it is not an ideal. In the welfare state, the unemployed are allowed to participate in society through consumption, while it is their human vocation to participate in society also through production. In the welfare state, the unemployed passively wait for their money; they are deprived of creative participation, and they easily lose their sense of membership in society. They are tempted to concentrate on themselves and their own trouble. What is required, according to the papal theory, is a new division of labour that will allow all members of society to labour, to share in production. This is the key to the difficulties raised.

The call for full employment, then, does not demand that society endlessly increase the production of goods. Even without spectacular growth, it should be possible to put all people to work if we include in the concept of productive labour the building of society and its qualitative transformation. All could be employed if we wanted to repair our cities, cultivate the countryside, renew our systems of transportation, care for children, the sick and the aged, change the quality of social communication and improve the conditions of public life. All people could become involved in building the society to which they belong; and if all labour, they all deserve to make a living from their work. This argument, it must be emphasized, is not made to justify the dismantling of the welfare system existing at this time. On the contrary, it implies an alternative vision of the economy, one that is within reach of contemporary society, if only the use of capital could be democratically controlled.

This emphasis on the dignity of labour, on labour as the source of human dignity, does indeed promote a kind of work ethic, not a work ethic that makes people work hard from a sense of duty or from a desire to succeed or from a longing for personal wealth, but a work ethic that allows people to experience their participation in Creation. It is a work ethic with the accent on the subject, on the transformation of personal consciousness. Play and leisure have their important role, but precisely as pauses of restoration in a life dedicated to the building of a just and peaceful community. Nor is this particular work ethic opposed to contemplation. There is in fact a contemplative dimension in work itself, man's proper self-realization. Moreover, reflection, prayer and quietude are necessary; without these, people suffer spiritual death. While there are forms of contemplation that introduce people to a realm separated from labour and historical responsibility, the spirituality recommended in *Laborem Exercens* intends to strengthen people so that they become ever more effectively the subjects of their history. Spirituality is meant to support people in their subjectivity. According to the encyclical, "The Church sees it as its particular duty to form a spirituality of work which will help people to come closer, *through work*, to God, Creator and Redeemer" (n. 24).

In the tradition of Western Christianity, prayer has never been totally separated from work. *Ora et labora* ("work and pray"), the motto of early Benedictine spirituality, has reasserted itself again and again in the life of the Church, its people and its religious orders. What is necessary, therefore, is to distinguish carefully between a work ethic that protects the contemplative dimension of human life and a work ethic that leaves no room for it—by despising inwardness, by deriving strength from guilt feelings, by making us into compulsives, or in some other way. The great spiritual writers of Protestantism praised the dedication of the simple craftsmen, farmers and merchants, whose work was conceived as a service to the community. For these writers, work and stewardship were intimately connected. Modern capitalist society has generated a work ethic of a different kind altogether.

What is the impact of the emphasis on the dignity of labour on people without jobs? Does it undermine their self-respect even more? What is more likely is that this emphasis will make the unemployed angry with an economic system that excludes them, and will generate motivation for political and social action. Some new theories that predict the restriction of labour to a few hours a week, and hence the arrival of a new age of leisure, appear, in the light of the encyclical, as ideologies designed to pacify the unemployed, present them as heralds of a new culture, and thus reconcile them with a situation of grave injustice. The bishops' call for full employment, then, is most appropriate both from a practical and from a pastoral point of view.

The International Dimension

A third objection raised first by religious and later by secular critics touches upon the lack of attention given by the New Year's Statement to international relations and the economic problems of the Third World. Father Bill Ryan offered an evaluation of the New Year's Statement a few weeks after its publication. While Father Ryan stood behind the bishops' statement, he made a few critical remarks, including the substantial observation that the problems of the Third World had been forgotten. In concentrating on their critique of foreign ownership and the demand for more self-reliant economic development in Canada, the bishops had neglected the grave situation created by foreign ownership and foreign control in the less developed nations. If

Canada aims at a self-reliant economy, does this mean that it will not buy textiles and other goods that are just beginning to be produced by Third World nations?

The statement does not raise this issue. This is undoubtedly an oversight. Other pastoral statements made by the Canadian bishops have mentioned the international dimension of the new economic order.[31] Papal social teachings, especially Paul VI's *Populorum Progressio* and John Paul II's *Laborem Exercens*, put great emphasis on the international responsibility of the developed nations and urge that their economic policies include support for the struggling economies of the poor nations. The international dimension, one might add, is a characteristic of Catholic social teaching, reflecting the international nature of the Catholic Church.

The New Year's Statement does analyze the crisis of international capitalism and points to the problems created by the unchecked power of the transnationals. But then it forgets this aspect when it formulates the proposals for a new economic orientation. Father Bill Ryan thinks that the Canadian bishops are too optimistic in their assumption that governments are still in a position to control the national economy and that the Keynesian policies that worked so well in the past are still workable. He suggests that in many areas of the economy the transnationals have acquired such power that government is obliged to serve their interests if it wants to keep industries in the country at all. The United Nations may well be correct when it demands a new, *international* economic order that will release the poorer countries from the grip of foreign capital and demand significant concessions or sacrifices from the developed nations.

This omission does not invalidate the statement. There is no reason why Canada could not strive for a more self-reliant economy and at the same time be a reliable customer of less developed nations and be bound by international contracts involving specified goods produced by them. In the handbook, *Witness to Justice*, published by the Social Affairs Commission of the CCCB, the international responsibility of Canadian society is given extended attention.[32]

Conclusion

We have seen that the New Year's Statement of the Canadian bishops is in perfect continuity with the Church's social teaching, in particular with its recent trend, and that it represents a high point of a development that has taken place in the Canadian Catholic Church. In fact, the meaning of the statement cannot properly be understood unless it is read in this historical context. The encyclical *Laborem Exercens*, moreover, is an important key for understanding some of the points made in it.

What is the power of the bishops' statement in Canada? There can be no doubt that its impact has been extraordinary. It has released a public debate in which all sectors of society became involved. It was regarded as an important document outside the Catholic community. Even the people who disagreed with the statement's orientation have for the most part responded to it in dignified fashion, recognizing the importance of the ethical perspective. But what is the power of the statement in the

Catholic community? Gone are the days when Catholics simply followed the directives given them by their bishops. In the area of social teaching in particular, Catholics have never shown a strong inclination to follow the Catholic tradition. In that area Catholics on the whole tend to follow the political and social ideals mediated to them by their culture. The great majority of Catholics who take their religion seriously are inclined to regard social justice concerns as a secular issue. They have been taught to understand the Christian message as having to do with personal salvation and holiness, with God's grace in the Church. Catholics who have had the new religious experience discussed in this commentary, a religious experience that reveals the emancipatory thrust of the Gospel, are a minority. Those Catholics rejoiced in the New Year's Statement. The impact of this statement in the Church and in Canadian society depends, therefore, on the people, be they Catholic or not, who pick it up and travel with it. The statement will exert significant influence on Canadian society if committed people make it the starting point of an ongoing debate, if they organize study groups, panel discussions and action committees that try to spell out, in imaginative fashion, the many ways in which the statement may be applied to the problems of Canadian society. This commentary has been written as a contribution to such a course of action.

3
Do Canada's Bishops Make Economic Sense?

Duncan Cameron

As Canadians prepared to welcome 1983, many among us were without work. For the jobless, the traditional New Year's celebration, at its best an expression of human fellowship—through a round of parties, drinks, midnight suppers and songs—would be small consolation for the reality of a day-to-day existence without gainful employment. For the unemployed, the indignity of a New Year's Day headache was a better expression of their situation than an evening of fun. Without either reason to celebrate or means to entertain, Canada's job seekers faced the worst economic January since the Great Depression of the 1930s.

Government and business leaders blamed inflation for economic difficulties. Inflation led to unemployment, closed factories and made consumers reluctant to spend. Speaking to the Canadian Club of Toronto in November, the governor of the Bank of Canada expressed, once again, the dominant government and business view: until inflation was beaten, interest rates would stay high, and prospects for economic recovery would remain dim.[1]

Perhaps surprisingly, the strongest, clearest

statement of dissent from the prevailing consensus came not from Parliament, provincial legislatures, business, labour or political economists. It came from the Canadian Conference of Catholic Bishops. In its New Year's Statement, "Ethical Reflections on the Economic Crisis," the Episcopal Commission for Social Affairs argued that unemployment, and not inflation, should be recognized as Canada's number one problem.

By taking this position, the bishops called into question the official view, not only in Canada, but in other industrialized countries as well. At the economic summit of Venice in 1980, the leaders of the seven major countries meeting declared that reducing inflation was the first priority. Though unemployment was a growing concern—and this was reflected in subsequent summit declarations of Ottawa (1981) and Versailles (1982)—the economic policies followed by the summit countries, with the exception of France, which for a time stressed the need for additional employment, were aimed at first reducing inflation.

The prime minister of Canada reacted to the bishops' statement by questioning their credentials as economists. The finance minister suggested that Canadian economists would surely reply to the case made by the report, which he noted did not seem to have the support of all Canadian bishops. Yet the Social Affairs Commission report received accolades from professional economists, as well as criticism. And other Christian groups lined up behind the Catholic bishops in defence of the document. The primate of the Anglican Church of Canada said, "the bishops didn't overstate the serious consequences of unemployment."[2] In

Quebec, fourteen Christian groups came together to declare their "solidarity with the propositions of the Bishops concerning the economic crisis."[3]

One goal of the report was to provoke dialogue and debate over what was called "a deepening moral disorder in the values and priorities of our society." The bishops called for discussion on major issues of economic justice, and they have not been disappointed. Amidst the controversy that followed the release of the document, with the strong negative reactions from some business groups and editorialists, and the expressions of support from other groups, including the labour movement, it remains difficult for many Canadians to come to grips with the economic issues raised by the bishops. Though it is not simply a question of whether on economic matters we should listen to bishops and labour leaders or accept the views of conventional economists and business executives, there remains a fundamental question: Who can be believed? And why?

Finding answers to controversial questions is never easy, but they can be answered. This commentary is designed to help those who are concerned with the issues raised by the bishops to make up their own minds—both on the merits of the positions being argued and with respect to the reasons for accepting or refusing the arguments themselves. Ultimately the answer to the question—who can be believed?—lies, in a democracy of the type Canada aspires to be, with ourselves.

A fundamental democratic belief is that areas of common concern should be subject to common consideration. While government and business leaders may agree on the best course for policy, it is only when Canadians accept to go along that dominant views become a consensus. For this reason it is important to Canadian democracy that informed public opinion provide the context for controversy and debate. Otherwise, on matters of collective interest, decisions are imposed by default.

In order to assess whether anti-inflationary strategies have produced social and moral disorder, as suggested by the New Year's Statement, this commentary begins by examining the fight against inflation. Monetary and wage restraint—the principal policies chosen by government—are contrasted with the price and profit controls suggested by the bishops. It is seen that the anti-inflationary strategy had a destructive impact on the economy and that, as argued by the bishops, low-income and unemployed Canadians were victims of government policy. Indeed, since much of the controversy surrounding the bishops' statement has to do with their claim that in the attempt to restore profits the unemployed are being sacrified, the second section of this commentary looks at the costs of unemployment.

But the bishops do not simply condemn unemployment; they offer an analysis of economic crisis. As will be seen here in the third section, they criticize Canadian strategies for economic recovery because these perpetuate the problems that are at the heart of the current crisis. The fourth section of this commentary explores the new approaches called for by the bishops, approaches that suggest alternatives to the dominant economic model that governs our society and that would reorder values and priorities in economic life. In the conclusion some of the political questions raised by "Ethical Reflections" will be examined.

Fighting Inflation: The Costs of Monetarism and Wage Restraint

One theme runs like a thread through the various criticisms of the bishops' statement. It is that the report underestimates the dangers to society in general and democracy in particular of inflation. The bishops are said to have misunderstood the links between anti-inflationary policies and unemployment.[4] Yet few would contest that the priority attached to fighting inflation by governments and business, a priority which led to economic policies of "monetarism" being adopted in most Western nations, has produced hardship. Rather than the traditional commitment to full employment guiding public policy, the new orthodoxy in recent years has countenanced higher unemployment so that price increases would be restricted. It is no exaggeration to say that governments have deliberately allowed unemployment to rise as an anti-inflationary measure. For the bishops, inflation is something to be controlled, but not through policies that put people out of work.

Orthodox business and government thinking has viewed the inflationary excesses of the late 1970s as akin to a disease infecting Western societies. This sickness had to be purged or democracy itself could be its victim. The usual historical analogy used to demonstrate the danger of inflation is the experience of hyperinflation in Germany at the time of the Weimar Republic, which is held to have contributed to the rise of fascism. It is argued that the basis for democracy is a middle class of property owners, and that since inflation erodes the value of property, it weakens the middle class. By appealing to the desire for stability and invoking the threat of monetary collapse unless disciplinary measures are introduced, governments are able to present anti-inflationary programs as a sort of bad-tasting medicine.

The message that accompanied monetarism was short-term pain for long-term gain. High interest rates today would lead to lower inflationary increases before too long, and be followed by economic recovery based on increases in private sector investment. All would agree that monetarism did produce pain. The real question is whether it is short-term pain or whether it has produced permanent damage as well. In order to understand the implications of the monetarist strategy, it is important to look at the circumstances that led to its introduction in the Western world.

One of the reasons monetarism was widely accepted was its simplicity: it could be easily understood and explained. In essence, monetarism suggested that the rate of increase in inflation was directly linked to the supply of money in the economy. If the money supply increased more rapidly than the increase in the supply of goods and services to the market, then the extra money would bid up prices, thus causing inflation.

The adoption of monetarist policies, then, meant that targets were established for growth of the money supply. Rather than attempt to stabilize interest rates, the traditional role of monetary policy, central banks allowed interest rates to rise as monetary growth was restricted. In Canada the monetary authorities began controlling the narrowly based money supply (demand deposits and currency, or M1) in 1975; but the strict monetarist experiment was abandoned by 1980 when external pressures on the Canadian dollar focused attention on the rate of interest needed to finance the current account deficit. This produced even higher interest rates.

Monetarism meant that money lenders received a higher return on their money. The inflation of the 1970s had eroded the value of monetary assets. Price increases outstripped the income growth of money lent at prevailing interest rates, thus producing a negative real rate of return on loans. However, by 1979 severe restrictions on monetary growth in the seven summit countries provided lenders with positive rates of return. Indeed, for 1981 the International Monetary Fund (IMF) calculated real interest rates as averaging 4.5 per cent in the seven major economies.[5] One result was higher returns on financial instruments, but others included recession, increased unemployment, downward pressure on wages, and a debt crisis in the Third World. If inflation had benefited borrowers who had purchased real assets and producers of commodities that had increased in price, monetary restriction squeezed borrowers in order to restore the balance sheets of lenders, and in the process slowed production and sales of goods and services, and indirectly restrained price increases.

Monetarist policies contributed directly to the worst economic conditions since the Depression of the 1930s. It was the deliberate character of this "made-by-government" recession that led the bishops to state publicly their disagreement with government policies. The bishops argued that by acting to protect the value of capital, even at the expense of creating unemployment, governments and the societies that elected them revealed a bias against the interests of labour.

The anti-inflationary strategies adopted in Canada were not limited to monetarism and high interest rates. Governments acted directly to control public service wages, and by doing so, revoked agreements that had been freely negotiated. Contracts for work were torn up, while contracts to pay interest on bonds were sacrosanct. Private sector employers were encouraged to impose similar salary restrictions, in the belief that by reducing business costs, lower wages led to increased investment. Work demands mental and physical toil; yet this human exertion was treated as if it were less important than interest paid to lenders or profits of business.

The bishops called for direct controls on prices and profits. They suggested that wage-restraint programs that imposed the same control rates on upper incomes as on lower incomes were inequitable. An economic recovery strategy that emphasized the fight against inflation led to layoffs and cutbacks in social services as well as wage restraint. The New Year's Statement found that "there are no clear reasons to believe that working people will ever really benefit from these and other sacrifices they are called to make."

Certainly, anti-inflationary measures had the generous support of business leaders. Public opinion polls showed that a majority of Canadians were deeply concerned about inflation. It could be expected that governments would act to curb price increases. But was it reasonable to think that lower wages, social spending restrictions and unemployment were necessary in order for economic prosperity to return to Canada?

The only way to judge the anti-inflationary strategy is to look closely at the question of inflation. What are its causes and how can it be controlled? The subject is controversial, but like most of the issues raised by the bishops, it goes beyond the realm of economics as such. Inflation is first and foremost a social and political question.

Inflation is normally conceived as a persistent increase in the average level of prices as measured by the consumer price index (CPI) or some other aggregate measure. At first glance one might assume that so long as increases in income keep pace with price increases, inflation is not a direct threat to prosperity. However, the problem with this view is that if prices rise faster in Canada than in other countries (particularly the U.S., which is Canada's largest trading partner by far), then Canadians will buy more lower-cost goods from abroad and sell less higher-cost Canadian goods. The business argument that inflation in Canada (if it is worse than in countries with which we trade) will cause unemployment makes sense, since Canadian firms will become less competitive, sell less goods and employ fewer people. But the business view of the consequence for Canadian trade and employment of inflation goes further than a simple denunciation of price increases. It singles out labour costs as the primary factor leading to price increases and generally supports wage restraint in order to secure Canada's international competitive position.[6]

There are a number of problems with the idea that it is wages that determine the international competitiveness of Canadian goods and services. First, many export prices are set in the international marketplace. This is particularly true for industrial raw materials and agricultural commodities, which make up a large percentage of Canadian exports. For these goods, labour costs are an insignificant element in calculating prices.

Second, most Canadian goods and services are priced for sale abroad in U.S. dollars, not Canadian dollars. This means that our international competitive position depends on our exchange rate. Some observers would go so far as to claim that our flexible exchange rate permits us to adjust the external value of our dollar to maintain a competitive position. Since the Canadian dollar has fallen against the U.S. dollar in recent years, this has given our exporters a dividend. Their costs are paid in Canadian dollars, but their revenues are received in U.S. dollars. While workers are expected to reduce their wage demands to help sales abroad, seldom, if ever, are they offered additional compensation when windfall profits occur.

Third, if one takes at face value the proposition that wage costs determine export competitiveness, one would have to conclude that high-wage economies like Canada, West Germany, Holland and the U.S. can never compete with the low-wage areas of the Third World. Either our wages will have to adjust to Third World levels or jobs will be exported to low-wage countries. The fact that high-wage economies can also be successful exporters means that factors other than wages are involved in competition. All things being equal, wages may be a determining factor in prices and competitivness, but all things are not equal in international trade. Endowments of natural resources, proximity to markets, service provided to clients, and many other factors determine export performance as well.

The policy prescription of wage controls to increase exports is also somewhat in contradiction with the widely held view that international trade should be conducted under conditions of free access to overseas markets on terms equal to those prevailing for local firms. It is difficult to resist the conclusion that wage controls are a form of protectionism. And protectionism has long been identified by economists as a barrier to economic prosperity. By creating artificial advantages for Canadian producers, through sacrifices imposed on Canadian workers, ultimately the benefits of international trade are being thwarted.

In their report the bishops attach importance to the role of monopoly pricing in propagating inflation. By singling out this aspect of economic organization for attention, the New Year's Statement made many commentators uneasy. Yet it cannot be denied that monopolies exist and that by definition they set prices without being subject to the sort of market discipline that the economic textbook model lays out as a standard feature of reality. The bishops call for monopoly prices to be controlled directly, rather than indirectly through monetary and wage restraint.

The first monopoly suppliers of importance in our economy are, of course, governments at all levels. We are familiar with the influence of governments over prices for cigarettes, spirits, wines and beer, postage stamps, gasoline, heating oil, bus tickets, airplane tickets, railway rates of all kinds, and so on. In addition, through the imposition of taxes, governments also set prices for government services. Statistics Canada figures show that government price increases are an important component of increases in the CPI.[7]

In the so-called market sector of the economy, pricing decisions are subject to monopoly effects as well. The standard procedure for firms that have dominant market positions within a given industry is to estimate costs, plus a margin for profits, and using sales projections, they then set prices. This is the policy followed by an automobile producer, for instance. Of course, final prices may vary according to movements in demand, but the fundamental reality remains that of an economy in which very large firms are able to set wholesale prices rather than take the price the market sets for them. Under these circumstances, it is the ability of large firms to pass on cost increases to consumers and customers that leads to what observers call the inflationary spiral.

The costs incurred by large firms include raw material and other commodity costs, taxes and diverse government charges, import expenditures, equipment, heat, lighting and other building expenses, financial charges and labour costs. Increases in any of these component costs will probably lead to price increases unless overall costs of producing goods or services fall through innovation, technological change or an increase in labour productivity. Even in this event, there is no guarantee that cost decreases will be passed on to the consumer.

It has been argued that the existence of labour unions, which bargain with management over wages and salaries in a closed-shop environment, indicates monopoly pricing by labour.[8] However, it should be pointed out that only about three million Canadians belong to affiliated labour unions. This means that about 75 per cent of the labour force is not unionized. In fact, unemployed Canadians (two million) represent about 66 per cent of the strength of organized labour. Thus, for every twelve workers, three are unionized, two are unemployed, and seven are not represented collectively in wage and salary negotiations.

Labour unions are effective in securing compensation for cost-of-living increases through the collective-bargaining process. But it is difficult to attribute to unions the price increases in heating oil, imported goods, housing, food and the interest rate hikes, which have accounted for much of the rise in consumer prices in recent years. Rather it would seem that labour unions have some countervailing power; they can restore to their members salary lost to inflation. However, even this ability disappears in times of recession and corporate difficulties.

The economic problems, like monopoly pricing, that the New Year's Statement sees as structural difficulties in Western economies were intensified by the monetarist strategies designed to curb inflation. It is interesting to note how the corporate community responded to higher interest rates. One of the first effects of rising interest rates is for money to shift from the stock market to monetary instruments like term deposits. This causes some stock prices to fall below the value that they represent in terms of assets per share. Such companies become takeover targets. That is to say, control of operations can be purchased through transactions involving shares bought with borrowed money. The idea is that the future earnings that the shares represent can be applied to repay the cost of the loan. Capital appreciation of the share value can also be anticipated.

When stock prices were depressed by higher interest rates, it was very attractive to some major companies to acquire competitors or complementary operations.[9] Canadian Pacific, for instance, was encouraged to take over Canadian International Paper, in what at the time was the largest corporate transaction of this type. The transaction was financed by the banking community, at a cost of some $2 billion. Yet this type of transaction created not one job and indeed led to the "rationalization" of the operations of the two firms, which meant plant closures and layoffs, and rebounded into distress for the affected communities in the Ottawa Valley.

Moreover, in many instances the takeover fever that hit the Canadian business community turned out to produce financial hardship. As the recession deepened and interest rates continued to rise, the combination of falling earnings per share of the acquired company and increased costs of servicing the takeover loans, most of which were negotiated at floating rates that followed the market upwards, meant that companies were hard pressed to pay for the acquisitions. Their own depleted earnings were tied up in the now expensive takeover operations. This stifled investment in new production. The merger of production facilities as a result of takeovers led to increases in rates of underutilized industrial capacity, which further restrained investment. Moreover, in power struggles, business energy was dissipated, and corporate effort diverted away from innovative activity.

All Canadian business suffered from soaring debt charges, and the usual response was to reduce inventories, lay off workers, and cut expenditures. Thus, in 1981 the recession deepened into something approaching a depression. Ultimately, as the gross national product (GNP) declined and unemployment increased, price increases began to slow. Monetarism was successful in limiting inflation, but the cost to Canadians was steep. As large firms became larger by absorbing other firms, the degree of concentration of ownership increased. The tendency to large-monopoly and oligopoly structure in Canadian industry was reinforced. Companies disappeared and jobs were eliminated.

In the months following the bishops' report, the rate of inflation in Canada fell sharply. Some attribute this to the 6-and-5 wage-restraint program; others see this as the inevitable result of falling inflation in the United States. But it has always been the case that if recession is deep enough and unemployment high enough, the level of spending will no longer support price increases. In Canada, high interest rates choked consumer and investment spending, and increased unemployment. It is hard to argue with the bishops' view that the 1981-82 recession was in large measure a result of a government policy, and monetary policy in particular.[10]

Continued government spending, despite reduced government revenues resulting from a declining national income, provided a cushion for an economy that would otherwise have fallen further into depression than it did. However, it was often argued that government deficits were an obstacle to lasting economic recovery because large borrowings by the public sector kept up interest rates and "crowded out" private sector borrowers.[11] Most provincial governments did indeed introduce restraint programs to reduce deficits; but the federal authorities, while also practising restraint, saw their budget deficit grow as a result of recession which simultaneously caused increases in government spending and reduced revenue.

The great constraint on new government spending was then said to be the growing deficits. However, any attempt to reduce government spending would further weaken the economy, and probably further reduce revenue, and thus *increase* the deficit. Therefore, fiscal austerity was recognized to be self-defeating, at least by the federal government, which by October 1982 was predicting a budget deficit of $23.6 billion. But new job-creation programs were modest. Only about 40,000 new jobs (over two years) were promised in the April 1983 budget, despite a projected deficit for the fiscal year 1983-84 of $31.3 billion. And comprehensive industrial policies were rejected, since they were more likely to invite opposition than support from industry itself. The new Liberal finance minster did, however, reduce business taxes by $1.9 billion (over two years) while increasing consumer taxes.

The prevailing anti-inflationary consensus was a political success. Social responsibilities of government are now considered to be less legitimate, since government spending is believed to cause inflation. Monetarism and wage restraint may have produced personal hardship but were necessary for economic recovery. The bishops' "Ethical Reflections" challenges this new orthodoxy directly.

The Costs of Unemployment

The Canadian bishops condemn unemployment as socially unacceptable and as a scourge on our society. They believe high current levels of unemployment reveal that Canada suffers from a moral disorder.

Their argument is based on Christian values: that preference be given to the needs of the poor; that the rights of workers are more important than the maximization of profits; and that the participation of marginalized groups takes precedence over the preservation of a system that excludes them. The bishops' analysis is based on firsthand contact with Canadians. They conclude that our economy is in serious trouble. Our industrial and manufacturing capacity is shrinking, causing social dislocation and personal tragedy. They reject the consensus view that priority should be given to fighting inflation.

An assessment of the significance of the report should establish the magnitude of our economic difficulties. Is the economic crisis centred on unemployment rather than inflation? Does this crisis reflect the limits of current policies and strategies advanced by governments and corporations? Unless on these two points the bishops can be shown to be accurate, their report can be easily dismissed as irrelevant.

As evidence that the Canadian economy is in serious difficulty, the bishops rely mainly on illustrations of specific types of economic distress. The report depicts Canada at a time of factory shutdowns, worker layoffs and abandoned one-industry towns. Though one would have to be either quite obtuse or near-sighted to deny that Canadian society is experiencing trouble, as the bishops' report shows, it remains that for their depiction to be taken seriously, for the economic crisis facing Canada to be recognized, the unemployment dimension deserves fuller treatment than is offered by the report.

In a major study *Le Plein emploi: Pourquoi?* two Quebec economists have estimated the cost to Canadian society of unemployment.[12] According to Diane Bellemare and Lise Poulin-Simon, in 1981 the direct cost of maintaining some sort of income support for the unemployed was equal to 1.1 per cent of GNP, or $3.8 billion. But the *indirect* cost of unemployment in terms of lost revenue for governments, business, workers and the unemployed themselves was an amazing 12.3 per cent of GNP, or $40.4 billion. This compares with indirect costs of unemployment of 1.8 per cent of GNP in 1967 when unemployment was much lower. The authors conclude that unemployment is not simply a problem for the unemployed—all of Canadian society suffers. They point to low-unemployment countries such as Sweden, Austria and Japan, which practise full employment policies, as evidence that full employment is attainable. They suggest that full employment is a collective good which requires the participation of all social groups if it is to be achieved.

The Canadian population (civilian aged fifteen and over) was 18.7 million in January of 1983. The civilian labour force was 11.7 million. Thus, about 62 per cent of the adult population was considered to be part of the official work force: those working for pay or actively seeking paid work. This work force participation rate was up from 57.8 per cent in 1970, but down from an historic high of recent years of 67.2 per cent in July of 1981.

For statistical purposes, the Canadian labour force is divided into two groups: employed and unemployed. The official unemployment rate measures the number of job *seekers* as a percentage of the civilian labour force. While from 1970 to 1975 the unemployment rate averaged about 6 per cent, by January of 1983 it stood at 13.7 per cent.

The unemployment statistics are not entirely satisfactory as a measure of the number of Canadians willing to work but without a job. Though the unemployment trend does indicate, as well as any other statistical measure, the general economic performance, the number of unemployed Canadians is larger than the official statistics show. Recent data from Statistics Canada suggests that variations in the participation rate are partially due to the "discouraged worker" syndrome. People who have given up actively seeking work are not considered as unemployed. Officially they are classified as having left the work force.

Statistics Canada is providing an estimate of these discouraged workers. In addition, it is now estimating the number of people who are underemployed: working part-time but looking for a full-time job. Since a person is classified as employed even if he or she works only one hour during the week covered by a job survey, the employment statistics are no more accurate than the unemployment statistics. Among the underemployed workers were a disproportionate number of women. In June 1983 some 82,000 Canadians were considered by Statistics Canada to be discouraged workers and about 518,000 were considered as underemployed. In addition, the number of officially unemployed workers stood at 1.45 million. Over 50 per cent had been unemployed for more than fourteen weeks.[13]

Government leaders have argued that Canada has been creating jobs rapidly, more rapidly in fact than other industrialized countries. According to them, the problem of unemployment is explained first by the increasing participation rate, and in particular the number of women seeking full-time employment, and second by the recession, which has affected employment levels in all countries.[14] The bishops' report, while not denying that unemployment is an international problem or claiming that it is unique to Canada, refuses to accept that unemployment can be considered as a problem like other economic problems.

For the bishops, an economy that does not have as its *raison d'être* employment for all who are willing to work is morally unacceptable. Rather than explaining unemployment through a rise in the number of women entering the labour force, the bishops want to know why Canadians have, collectively, through their elected representatives, accepted the growing levels of unemployment of recent years.

If one adds together Statistics Canada estimates of discouraged workers, underemployed and officially unemployed, the number of Canadians without regular employment in June of 1983 was 2.05 million, or about 17 per cent of the work force. Even if only the officially unemployed are considered, and if the figures are broken down by age groups, a picture of unemployment emerges that presents a bleak future for young Canadians and their families. From June of 1982, the seasonally adjusted rate of unemployment for persons between the ages of fifteen and twenty-four has been in excess of 20 per cent. The jobless rate for recent school graduates seeking full-time employment was 26.4 per cent by May 1983.

It is sometimes argued that the unemployment problem is due to excessive benefits paid to the unemployed that induce laziness or a contempt for work.[15] It should be noted that a person who has never held a full-time job has recourse to provincial welfare payments rather than federal unemployment insurance (UI). A young single person in the province of Quebec receives less than $150 per month in welfare. This can hardly be considered an inducement not to work. As for UI payments, while they are substantial, they are designed to deal with cyclical variation in employment; that is to say, they protect people who have lost work, for a period up to one year, until they find work. People who have not been fired or laid off, but leave a job for which they may be unsuited, are disqualified for six weeks (above the two-week waiting period) from collecting UI benefits. Since benefits eventually run out, many formerly employed people end up on welfare. Rather than being an inducement not to work, UI probably has the effect of forcing people to stay in jobs they would otherwise find intolerable.

No one has seriously argued that unemployment is not a problem. Some observers have spoken of voluntary unemployment—that is, a number of the unemployed are expressing a preference not to work or a taste for leisure rather than income—but this tendency, if it exists, can hardly be expected to explain the swollen jobless rate. If one compares the number of job openings with the number of job seekers (about twenty jobless for each opening), it becomes immediately evident that the principal explanation for unemployment is no work for willing workers—unless, of course, one prefers to speak of too many workers. Temporary bulges in the work force, that is, an increasing participation rate, have occurred, but to argue that this explains unemployment is to neglect the more significant aspect of the question: the trend in employment.

Looking at the labour market picture in Canada over recent years, one set of figures appears most pertinent. Between 1973 and 1983, the number of Canadians employed in the goods-producing industries (forestry, fishing, trapping, mining, milling, manufacturing and construction) actually declined in absolute terms from 2.4 million to 2.3 million. Goods-producing industries provided employment for 19 per cent of the Canadian labour force in 1982 as opposed to 25 per cent in 1973. This decline of 6 per cent just about equals the 5.5 per cent increase in average unemployment in the same period (from 5.5 per cent in 1973 to 11 per cent in 1982).

The unemployment problem is firstly an employment problem. There are not enough jobs. The rise in employment in the service-producing industries (transportation, communication, utilities, trade, finance, insurance, real estate, public administration, defence, and commercial and non-commercial services) has not been sufficient to offset the decline in employment in goods-producing industries.

The number of jobs in goods-producing industries declined in every category except mining from 1973 to 1982. While the jobs available in services increased in every category over the same period, and some 6.54 million Canadians were employed in that sector by 1982 compared to 4.99 million in 1973, the nature of work in services is quite different from work in the goods-producing sector.

Recent evidence shows that the work force in North America is polarizing.[16] More jobs at the top of the income scale and at the bottom, less in the middle. This may partially explain why the distribution of income in Canada has remained uneven, despite some attempts at progressive taxation and increased social spending by governments. As the number of middle-income jobs declines and the number of low-paying jobs in services increases, the overall distribution of income continues to favour the higher earners. As the bishops point out, the top 20 per cent receive 42.5 per cent of personal income.

The statistical dimension of unemployment shows that it has attained serious proportions. Forecasts indicate that high unemployment will persist. According to Wood Gundy, Canada can do little more than increase employment by 1.5 per cent per year in the 1980s as compared with 2.75 per cent (on average) in the 1960s and 1970s.[17] What does this mean?

When Don Cherry was asked about being fired as a hockey coach, he replied: "I suddenly felt like a nobody." For him, unemployment was the discovery that his identity as a human being was given to him through his work. Without a team, he was no longer a hockey coach. Without a job, he no longer knew for sure what his life was about. Like other unemployed people, he still had skills, experience and knowledge. But without a chance to perform on the job and have his abilities recognized by others, he felt lost.

A temporary loss of employment is something that many Canadians have experienced (and that all hockey coaches expect). As viewers of "Hockey Night in Canada" know, Don Cherry got another job second-guessing other coaches for the CBC. But there are other unemployed Canadians whose loss of identity has not been temporary. The permanently unemployed or discouraged worker, in a society where we take meaning from what we do for a living, is the modern-day equivalent of a social outcast. The bishops enumerate the results of a troubled economy: "personal tragedies, emotional strain, loss of human dignity, family breakdown and even suicide."

The meaningful contact with others that comes with work is no longer available to unemployed people. As their self-esteem falls, they often suffer psychological difficulties. Studies done in Britain on the unemployed show that they tend to suffer from a disproportionate rate of physical illness as well.[18] In a letter to the newspaper *Le Devoir*, a researcher at the Université du Québec à Chicoutimi commented on a government decision to study suicide and alcoholism among the native population of Northern Quebec. "The results will probably show that alcoholism is due to genetic factors; but for those of us who knew the victims, it remains that not long ago they were working steadily, and not having problems with alcohol. Then they lost their jobs, started drinking, and suicide followed."[19]

In a society that assigns people social roles through their jobs, unemployment represents a denial of meaning to daily existence, and one should not be surprised to discover links between suicide and unemployment. While people can be protected, in part, from the financial indignities of unemployment, society cannot easily compensate the inability to express oneself through work. Without a job, people are dispossessed of their membership in society.

In recent years the definition of full employment has been changing. While in Canada 3 per cent unemployment was once considered to approximate full employment, some economists now talk about 5 or 6 per cent as unattainable given present economic conditions. It has been argued that the definition of full employment should be altered to take new social realities into account. Others, including the bishops, suggest that we think hard about what constitutes reality. Perhaps we need to change society rather than the definition of full employment.

While the bishops contend that anti-inflationary strategies of government and business have produced social and moral disorder, perhaps their main message is that even if these strategies are successful in their own terms (that is, in reducing inflation), they still fail in human terms. Because the society the strategies are meant to revive, is itself caught in structural crisis, measures that neglect this wider dimension are doomed to perpetuate the injustices of the current situation.

The Priority of Profit

For the bishops, the misguided campaign against inflation and the unemployment crisis are both symptomatic of a much larger structural crisis of international capitalism. They identify structural changes in both capital and technology that lead directly to unemployment.

Two arguments are advanced. First, according to the report, capital is becoming increasingly transnational; that is to say, investment moves from one country to another in response to lower taxes, cheaper labour or less stringent environmental regulations. This development has been referred to by scholars as a "new international division of labour."[20] The principal actors are transnational corporations (TNCs) and the major banks, which join together in syndicates to provide loans to TNCs. Indeed, the establishment of these world banking groups (WBGs) is one important aspect of the transnationalization process.

In essence, many of the standard products of the industrial age, such as steel, cars, ships, electric appliances and so on, can be produced in selected Third World countries at lower cost than in the Western nations. Production then moves offshore, leaving the so-called smokestack industries in the West to decline. The goods produced abroad are then sold back to the centre countries. The result may be reduced employment in the West coupled with an increase in employment, at lower wages, in the Third World. But the risk is that an overall decline in purchasing power may reduce the market for the offshore production, and the projected profits of transnational capital invested abroad may not be realized.

The second argument is that new investment in production is increasingly capital intensive: money goes into technology rather than salaries, equipment rather than jobs. Indeed, the purpose of high technology in the production process is to reduce unit costs so as to increase the productivity of invested capital.

The bishops imply no criticism of either investment in Third World nations or in advanced technology as such. Rather their concern is that either type of investment, while it may be profitable for some firms taken individually, may lead to an increase in unemployment and have the consequence of marginalizing more people within our society. What is being criticized is the basis on which investments are made and the fact that control over investment decisions by TNCs and WBGs may result in social costs that are unacceptable to Canadians. What is suggested is that the unrestrained search for profits by some may lead to generalized economic decline in which all suffer.

When business enterprises seek more output per worker, as has been the case in Canada, unless there is a mechanism for assigning any additional business revenues to job creation, lower levels of employment will result. Moreover, the bias against spending on salaries and in favour of spending on equipment means that less income is available for spending on consumer goods. A vicious circle results: lower consumer spending means that less consumer goods are produced; workers are then laid off, which further reduces spending, leading to lower production and yet more layoffs.

As well, some government spending is considered by the bishops to be biased against employment. One example given in the report is military spending. By assigning public monies to defence spending for technologically sophisticated equipment, government is transforming tax revenues, which are in large proportion taken from salaried Canadians, into arms production. Yet spending on military equipment produces less employment, and therefore less future tax revenue, than spending on, say, day-care centres. In a recession, spending on imported technology rather than on salaries, reduces the purchasing power of the community rather than raising it. It thwarts recovery rather than aiding it. Military hardware can hardly be considered to add to the stock of wealth of the community, since scarce resources are being spent on goods that will not produce other goods and require little human labour either to produce or to operate. By diverting money from taxes paid by individuals to military spending, governments contribute to structural unemployment.

The basis of Canadian economic policy has been to provide a climate in which the private sector is encouraged to invest. This investment will then, according to government thinking, lead to new jobs through economic growth. Conventional wisdom suggests that in order to invest, business must have profits, which amount to a sort of business savings. In this way of looking at the world, those factors that increase business costs, first reduce profits and subsequently reduce investment. It is this reasoning that led governments to introduce programs that encourage wage restraint.[21] Moreover, faced with large deficits, governments have been tempted to reduce social expenditures so that financial incentives to industry can be financed without raising taxes. Indeed, corporate leaders (who condemn government deficits) call for lower business taxes.

The increased international mobility of investment capital is cited as one factor that forces Canada to provide conditions for private investment and profits that are competitive with other countries. Accepting the logic of transnational investment means that Canada takes measures to enforce restraint, measures that might otherwise be unacceptable in a country which prides itself for the quality of its social programs and for the respect it accords to workers' rights, including the legal provisions for collective bargaining. In effect, under pressure from business leaders, the Canadian government passed Bill C-124, which broke existing collective agreements, took away the right to bargain collectively for more than 500,000 federal employees, and reduced the legal authority of public service unions to the point that their only remaining power was to process employees' grievances. The three major provincial governments of B.C., Ontario and Quebec all introduced similar measures, and much of private industry followed suit. The argument that the cost of government was a major impediment to private investment and that public sector wage levels influenced private sector wage settlements was invoked despite the fact that public sector wages had trailed inflation by 10 per cent since 1976.[22] A decline in real wages, which had already occurred, was being proposed by governments as a solution to recession!

The atmosphere surrounding relations between labour and management was hardly improved by the unilateral action by governments to restrict the freedoms of public sector labour unions. As the bishops point out, two consequences follow from the imposition of restraint programs. First, there is the danger that measures that deny traditional rights to bargain collectively and infringe upon acquired benefits of social programs, may be followed by additional authoritarian measures to enforce what amounts to restrictions of civil liberties. Second, the programs themselves may lead to social unrest, which could foreseeably call forth yet more authoritarian measures.

Perhaps the most controversial argument raised by the New Year's Statement is the contention that in present strategies for economic recovery, "the survival of capital takes priority over labour." By asserting the primary importance of restoring profits and investment, governments are "allowing people to be treated as an impersonal force having little or no significance beyond their economic purpose in the system."

It is the bishops' view that technology and capital are means to an end: the fulfillment of basic human needs. Current strategies, by focusing on measures that promote profits at the expense of wages in hopes of encouraging further investment, are unlikely to lead to economic recovery, since the business tendency to invest in labour-saving technology and to export capital would produce little or no new employment. By raising this point, the report strikes directly at economic policies in Western countries. If the analysis of the structural conflict between labour and capital is correct, the case against current policies is very strong indeed. And the conclusion that a moral crisis—the loss of human dignity—is in the making should be taken most seriously.

In the report, labour and capital are used as shorthand expressions to refer to the collective interests of different groups. Labour is considered to be those who earn their living from wages and salaries, and those who are willing to work but have no jobs. Capital refers to those whose income comes from ownership of capital assets: in the form of stock in corporations, privately held companies, or bonds and other debt instruments. Though some critics have found the terminology objectionable, so long as capital and labour are understood as sociological concepts, which define collective actors within society, the capital/labour distinction makes sense. Even the Income Tax Act uses it when it provides for different treatment of income depending on whether it comes from salaries and wages, or from interest, dividends, profits or capital gains.

Generally speaking, two types of criticism have been addressed to the use by the bishops of the capital-versus-labour perspective. First, some observers have argued that the bishops have neglected the serious difficulties facing business and, consequently, the owners of business. Second, it has been suggested that it is difficult to distinguish between the interests of workers, whose salaries depend on the success of private enterprise, and the owners of private enterprise. Therefore, the interests of capital and labour, rather than being antagonistic, are said to be complementary.[23]

While it is accurate to say that the statement does not focus on the difficulties that the economic crisis has imposed on corporations, and indeed the thrust of the report is that to equate business profits with economic well-being is misguided, the bishops do not neglect the impact of the crisis on corporations. The statement enumerates the various problems being created as business responds to declining profits. What the report does question is the view that there exists a global shortage of capital, as such, which inhibits new investment. The statement recognizes that while individual companies may be experiencing temporary shortages of investment capital, responding to this by laying off workers and reducing inventories, it is the perception by business that new investment will not be *sufficiently* profitable that holds back recovery.

What is considered indefensible by the bishops is the contradiction between the claim that only higher profits will restart the investment process and the reality of an economy suffering from sluggish investment *despite* idle funds. For the bishops, investment is needed to meet human needs and this takes priority over the desire of corporations for maximum profits. Can business's desire for higher profits through lower wages and taxes, plus the right to invest abroad and in labour-saving technology, be justified at a time of soaring unemployment and idle resources?

Business has argued that economic prosperity can be identified with profits precisely because it is profits that allow business to survive, grow, pay salaries and create jobs.[24] Without the profits that the marketplace confers on successful firms, there would be no motive to provide jobs for labour or management. This explains why sacrifices have to be made in order to provide the profits necessary for operation and expansion of business enterprises.

Without contesting the notion of profits, as such, the statement does dispute directly the contention that sacrifices should be made by the weak, poor, destitute or unemployed simply to increase *projected* profits. Rather the report suggests that sacrifices should be based on equity. The logical conclusion of this reasoning is that owners of capital have social responsibilities more important than the search for maximum profits. This means sacrificing the principle of profit maximization and accepting a relative decline in profits to preserve jobs.

What the report implies is that short-term profits cannot be considered the ultimate principle of economic organization, since short-term considerations have led to higher unemployment, which shows no sign of being temporary. The bishops clearly reject the notion of rising absolute profits as the major indicator of economic performance. They are concerned that increases in relative profits, at the expense of relative wages, impose an unjust burden on those who are the least able to assume that burden.

Where business finds its greatest point of disagreement with the report is in the contention that labour and capital are in conflict, that their interests are antagonistic rather than complementary. Most business representatives see corporations as forming a single entity that provides income for workers, management and shareholders.[25] They fail to see how workers can be considered to have interests ultimately separate from the firm that employs them.

The bishops view the question from another perspective. Their statement deplores an attitude favouring sacrifices by wage earners without giving labour a voice in the future of our economy. While the report does not question the fact that Canadians must together find a common response to the economic crisis (on the contrary, that is exactly the position adopted by the bishops), their report does cast serious doubt on propositions that neglect the unique ability of labour to produce wealth.

Within the standard business account of operations of industrial and commercial enterprises, it is assumed that owners and workers have different rights and responsibilities. By virtue of risks taken with ownership funds, shareholders are entitled to participate in profits. Salaried employees and wage earners are entitled to the fair market value of their work so long as the enterprise finds it profitable to employ them. The responsibility of management is to shareholders; the responsibility of workers is to management, as set out in an employment contract or collective agreement.

The business view of the economy suggests that the firm, or enterprise, justifies its own existence through its efficiency in providing needed goods and services at low costs. For society as a whole, the pursuit of profits through competition in the marketplace leads to an optimal allocation of scarce resources. It is the price mechanism that assigns values to factors of production (land, labour and capital) according to their relative scarcity. The market for final products brings together producers and consumers in an auction process in which consumer sovereignty rewards efficient production. It is the pursuit of profit, combined with freedom to buy and sell in the market, which assures that suppliers of land, labour and capital can obtain a maximum return, while producers are able to choose the combination of these factors that allows them to maximize efficiency and satisfy consumers.

This business view rests on the assumption that price adjustment in the market takes place under conditions of scarcity—responding to supply and demand—and that in this competitive process all participants are affected equally, in the sense that acting alone none can influence the market forces that determine prices. In short, it is suggested that the marketplace is neutral, and it is accepted that economic rewards are distributed according to justifiable criteria. The argument also assumes that economic activity can be considered productive when goods and services are offered for sale (and profit) in the market.

Many social scientists find the business view of the economy somewhat incomplete.[26] State institutions and government processes are neglected. The use of political power by major economic actors is ignored. Though government spending (all levels) amounts to nearly 50 per cent of Canadian GNP, most business observers persist in seeing governments as "unproductive" because they are outside the market. In particular, the important economic roles played by governments through public investment and investment guarantees provided for large, risky undertakings don't receive adequate attention in traditional explanations of the workings of the Canadian economy. Yet public investment has a long tradition in Canada, dating back to the 1820s in the case of the Lachine canal; and government investment guarantees were instrumental in the construction of the Canadian Pacific Railway.

A major critique of the conventional view of the economy was provided by John Maynard Keynes. His proposition was that the level of economic activity was determined by effective aggregate demand, and that investment determines savings, rather than savings determining investment. This implies that rather than past or present profits leading to investment, it is really the expected rate of profit that leads to investment. When the economy suffers from idle resources and unemployment, it is the result of weakness in consumer spending, exports, private investment or government spending, according to Keynes. In order to get the economy moving again, it is necessary to act directly on these variables; otherwise, stagnation will persist. Since conditions of falling wages and government restraint in the midst of international recession are unlikely to promote profit expectations, governments must take up the slack through public investment, financed through borrowing of idle funds. Though Keynesian economics remains controversial, its central argument—that an economy may stagnate at a level well below full employment due to the fundamental instability of private investment and spending—is generally accepted by economists. While some business groups accept the need for stimulative government spending, most reject the idea that it is investment that precedes profits and not profits that precede investment.

The business view that it is the markets and the price mechanism that regulate economic activity in an even-handed manner, is based more on belief than on observation of the economy. Large corporations, governments and trade unions have all demonstrated their ability to influence prices and dominate markets. A vision of an economy formed of households and firms, each incapable of affecting supply and demand, and therefore prices, ignores evidence of price setting by regulation, government fiat, monopoly and oligopoly. The tendency for prices to rise is a feature of the modern economy. If competitive market forces were fully operative, one could reasonably expect prices to fall with the same frequency and intensity as they rise. In fact, prices are "sticky." Other than for some raw materials and agricultural commodities, they tend not to fall. Most price movements are asymmetrical; they move up more than down.

Where the corporate vision of the economy is most at odds with the ideas put forward by the bishops is in respect to the way it portrays human beings either as consumers or as factors of production. Rather than see economic activity as providing material conditions to sustain a social life in which human values have priority, there is a tendency to transform the principles of market economics into ends in themselves. Instead of accepting that the economy is something fashioned by people to meet human needs, business representatives often use a language that implies that human beings must adapt themselves to the necessities of the marketplace. The use of the market analogy with respect to labour, to give one instance, leads to workers being thought of in the same terms as fresh produce.

The moral crisis identified in the New Year's Statement features an increasing domination of the weak by the strong, both at home and abroad. The bishops explicitly reject economic policies which are based on an appeal to the nineteenth-century doctrine of "survival of the fittest," known as social Darwinism. Pointing out that the poor nations of the Southern Hemisphere with 75 per cent of the world's population are expected to survive on less than 20 per cent of the world's income, the report suggests that under conditions of tough competition, the plight of the poor of the world can only worsen. The bishops see that policies based on the ability to dominate markets result in an increased concentration of wealth and power in the hands of a few. They believe that no good can possibly come of a situation where the survival of the fittest is offered as the supreme law of economics. In its place they call for technology and capital to be harnessed by society to meet basic human needs. The bishops speak of the development of peoples as being the basis for a more moral economic order.

By taking a public stand based on human values, the bishops have forced a public debate on the nature of the economy. Their analysis can be summarized in the contention that an economy that does not serve the human needs of the community is unacceptable. The decision to speak out against policies leading to domination and inequality reflects the commonly understood view that by remaining silent one consents to current policies.

Creating a Resilient Canadian Economy

In their report the bishops call for the adoption of specific new strategies by both government and business to deal with current economic problems. They suggest an industrial strategy—the creation of new labour-intensive industries to meet basic needs. Inflation should be attacked through price controls, taxes on investment income, and the more equitable distribution of wages. According to the report, social spending should remain a priority. Finally, they ask that labour unions be invited "to play a more decisive and responsible role in developing strategies for economic recovery and employment."

While recognizing that the crisis, as such, is deep-seated in nature and international in scope, the bishops hold out hope for the future. They believe "that people must indeed meet and work together as a true community in the face of the current economic crisis." When they state that "people must have a chance to choose their economic future rather than have one forced upon them," they are warning Canadians of the dangers inherent in policies formulated behind closed doors. The bishops call for explicit recognition that past policies have failed to help many people in the community and that future policies must be judged by their contribution to "the struggles for economic justice."

A report by the Ontario Manpower Commission forecasts that shortages of skilled workers will occur because Canadian industry is neglecting to train tool-and-die makers, general machinists, welders, wood patternmakers, millwrights and instrument mechanics, despite government subsidies that pay up to 75 per cent of a trainee's salary in the first year of a skills-development program and 50 per cent in the second year.[27] The report points out that Canadian corporations have traditionally imported from other countries up to 75 per cent of the skilled workers they employ. Before the recession there was considerable interest by industry in government-sponsored training, but applications for long-term programs reached only 1,800 apprentices in 1982 even though some 4,000 places were available. Short-term development was more popular with industry, and about $25 million was made available for 10,000 trainees.

Most job training occurs in the workplace. Unless people are able to acquire job experience, their chances of finding suitable employment are dim. The situation is classic "catch 22": in order to get a first job, you have to have held a job. Therefore, the unemployed, without experience, cannot find work, while the skilled and higher trained, who are employed, are in demand.

While the bishops criticize past policies for current employment shortages, it should be recognized that under prevailing economic practice, when even government subsidies have failed to entice industry to take on workers in significant numbers during hard times, new strategies must somehow address the economic system itself. Can the government stimulate the economy in the midst of a world recession without suffering the fate of the French, who saw imports rise while exports failed to respond, and suffered a financial crisis as a result of such a policy? Can direct job creation take place in an economy which measures success by profits, when new workers mean additional costs to an individual firm, which must then produce more goods or services even though it can't sell what is already produced?

The quick answer is no on both counts. Overall stimulation of a general nature is unlikely to produce a better future unless world economic conditions are already considered to be improving. Firms add workers when they have problems meeting demand, and lay them off when they have unsold products or services. Job-creation programs depend on the willingness of business to provide tools and materials for new workers. Faced with recession, they are unlikely to do so. The great barrier to recovery from recession or depression is that present capacity to produce is not being fully utilized. Since Canadian production had fallen to below 60 per cent of capacity by January 1983, there was no incentive to spend or invest.

Individual firms face the paradox that if they reduce costs, they improve projected profits; but if all firms reduce spending, actual profits are reduced. If all firms practise restraint, economic decline is cumulative. Under these circumstances, some public leadership is needed to improve economic conditions.

There are indications that Canada, like other Western nations, is facing a period of prolonged unemployment, which is unlikely to diminish significantly as a result of a cyclical upturn in the economy. Speaking to the Canada Tomorrow Conference in November 1983, Heather Menzies identified this phenomenon as "jobless economic growth." In this context, the policies that governments propose to apportion the burden of sacrifice and distribute the rewards of whatever economic recovery does occur, reflect their understanding of our society. As the bishops contend, economic questions reveal a moral and ethical dimension.

The first concern of business is with corporate survival. In difficult times, when prospects for recovery are tied to increased corporate profitability and where the primary responsibility of business is to its shareholders, is it sufficient to suggest that corporations will provide us with moral and ethical leadership?

It is difficult to avoid concluding that the bishops' message rejects the capitalist model that has guided our society. By contesting current strategies for recovery that favour profit maximization at the expense of workers' rights, the bishops are stating loud and clear that our present economic "rules of the game" are in need of change. By arguing for economic policies that give priority to the needs of the poor, rather than to the wants of the rich, the bishops have declared their dissatisfaction with the social order. By condemning a system which marginalizes certain groups within society, the bishops are saying that full participation of all must take precedence over political forms of representation that allow exclusion of some.

Criticism by the bishops of our society's dominant economic model leads them to propose a reordering of values and priorities. They suggest that a shift in values can be brought about through the adoption of alternative approaches to economic life. Interestingly, the bishops are far from rejecting economic growth as a social objective; rather, they propose alternative goals for economic growth.

The bishops are concerned that Canadian industries be self-sufficient, that manufacturing and construction industries be strengthened, that capital be made available to underdeveloped regions, that local communities receive new job-producing industries, and that job-training programs be provided. Taken together, these ideas represent an alternative to the economic strategy proposed by the Liberal government in its paper *Economic Development for Canada in the 1980's*, which focused on the benefits of megaprojects for Canadian industry.[28] Indeed, the bishops single out the corporate-based megaproject strategy (released with the 1981 budget) for criticism.

The government's view at that time was that Canadian resource development could be a leading sector for economic growth. Based on a study by a Major Projects Task Force, which identified some $440 billion in projected investment spending for individual projects having a value of $100 million or more, the government policy paper noted that an "area in which Canada is presented with exceptional economic development opportunities is manufacturing activity both to supply machinery, equipment, and materials needed for resource development and to extend the further processing of resource products beyond the primary stage."

The underlying assumptions of the government policy were that world demand for Canadian resource production would be strong and prices would rise because of international shortages. The areas in which investment spending was under consideration included energy, which accounted for the lion's share with 79 per cent, as well as agriculture, forest-based industry, and mining. It was considered that through state policies the 20 per cent of Canadian GNP generated in resource development could be linked to the 20 per cent of GNP accounted for by industrial manufacturing.

Obviously, the simultaneous development of energy resources on the scale envisaged by the Liberal government strategy entails the export of energy products. Though the National Energy Policy (NEP) posited self-sufficiency as a goal for energy production in Canada, the megaprojects strategy requires access on a continuing basis to overseas markets as an outlet for increased energy production; otherwise, the investment in energy production capacity could not be recovered. Of the projected spending on megaprojects, 17.8 per cent is accounted for by conventional hydrocarbon exploration and development, 9.7 per cent by heavy-oil development, 7.2 per cent by pipeline construction, and 45.3 per cent for electrical generation and transmission. This means massive investment in energy infrastructure, designed to produce and transport Canadian resources to ultimate purchasers, presumably in the U.S. for the most part because historically it represents our most important market for energy exports.

The key to the success of the policy lies in using Canadian materials, techniques, capacities and equipment to realize the megaprojects. The industrial benefits of development on the scale envisaged, if they could be captured by Canadian firms, would mean not only immediate stimulus to economic growth but as well provision for the future sales abroad of the megaproject capacities developed domestically. Once again it is presumed that international demand, as a result of buoyant world markets, would allow for penetration by Canadian industrial firms of foreign markets.

This supply-and-demand scenario, both for resources and related manufacturing capacity, has made the whole strategy extremely vulnerable to developments in the world economy. Since the release of the Liberal policy statement, the world market for oil production has softened. World demand for energy has declined both as a result of the recession and of the introduction of energy conservation measures in many countries. Without growth in the world economy, which the Canadian government is unable to guarantee and virtually unable to influence, the sale of resource production abroad is constrained and the megaprojects strategy is stalled. Without major recovery of world markets, the projected energy spending cannot be recouped through additional production, and the related development of industrial capability will not take place.

The great attraction of the megaprojects strategy was political. The projects initially identified by the task force were spread out across the country in a fashion that provided for regionally balanced economic development. In addition, labour unions were well represented on the task force. But the Liberal strategy was designed so that private investment would be the motor of growth. Understandably, since so far megaproject development does not appear profitable, private investment markets have not responded.

The role of government policy in the strategy was to provide support for private investors, principally large corporations, through the adoption of mechanisms of industrial adjustment: research and development subsidies, manpower training, tax incentives, and regional development grants. Indeed some $60 billion was set aside for these purposes for a five-year period commencing in 1981-82. But the deepening recession has slowed private investment spending of all sorts, and government policies appear ineffective, designed as they were to play only a supporting role. Megaprojects are seldom referred to by government these days; yet no major alternative strategy has been forthcoming from the state sector.

It is this gap in government policy, this lack of leadership, that the New Year's Statement finds deplorable. At a time of crisis, to be caught without a viable alternative to unemployment and welfare, is surely unacceptable. Equally unacceptable is an attitude of passivity when face to face with economic difficulties. Recognizing this, and anticipating criticism from areas of the country dependent on declining industries, the government has been putting in place mechanisms to deal with the so-called sunset industries. At the same time there has been much discussion of the "sunrise" sector of high technology, and government policies are emerging to deal with its development.

New policies for industrial adjustment and development, while lacking strategic coherence, do represent what the bishops refer to as an industrial vision. The goal is to increase the capacity of Canadian firms to compete on world markets.[29] An Industrial Renewal Board has been created to promote adaptation of traditional manufacturing enterprises in textiles, clothing and footwear. Every indication is that faced with competition from low-wage areas abroad, these industries are being encouraged to modernize production techniques; this means, of course, the elimination of labour-intensive production.

Yet the improvement of the international competiveness of Canadian industry will do nothing by itself to expand markets. The best that can be expected is to protect existing market shares. But at what cost? By increasing unemployment? By increased exploitation of workers?

In addition, without expansion in the world economy, any policies designed to promote exports can only succeed by displacing the exports or home production of other countries. Will our trading partners allow this to happen without adopting overtly protectionist policies? The evidence is that world trade is contracting (by 2 per cent in 1982) and that protectionist policies are on the rise. Indeed the Organization for Economic Cooperation and Development (OECD) has talked about protectionism as reaching crisis proportions.[30] In this context, is export promotion the best path to economic growth?

The regular injunctions from government leaders, business people and bankers for Canadians to tighten their belts, work harder and pull together to face tough international competition would lead us to believe that Canada is faring poorly in international trade. In fact, the Canadian merchandise trade balance is positive; Canadian exports exceed imports. A record trade surplus of nearly $18 billion was being recorded in 1982 at the same time as the prime minister warned prime-time television viewers about the dangerous inroads being made by foreign industry into Canadian markets at home and abroad. While it is the case that if trade in manufactured goods is considered apart from overall merchandise trade, Canada has shown deficits, it is reasonable to ask if our trading partners would allow us to reverse this situation in manufactured trade and further increase our overall surplus, without taking discriminatory action against our exports.

Historically Canada has been very successful in

international trade. Our merchandise trade balance has been positive in every year but one since 1960. Our balance of trade with the U.S. turned positive in 1968 and has remained positive since then in every year but one. If trade with the U.S. is excluded from consideration, our merchandise trade figures with the rest of the world show Canada to be a net exporter of merchandise in every year since 1946. Though no one would deny the importance of world trade to the Canadian economy, it can fairly be asked if the source of our economic difficulties does not more properly lie with the inability of Canadians to buy and sell goods and services from and to each other in sufficient quantities to ensure full employment rather than with our inability to export.

It is within this context that the bishops concern for a locally, and regionally, based industrial strategy can best be understood. The bishops argue, with cause, that attempts to promote yet more exports of resources (albeit in the hopes of reaping domestic industrial benefits) lead to imports of money and ownership capital, thus increasing Canada's foreign debt. Some foreign borrowing to finance resource production may make sense, since revenues are going to come from foreign markets. However, Canadian investment funds, private and public, are inevitably entwined with foreign funds in order to facilitate export production. The combination of high-cost foreign borrowing, weak overseas markets, and domestic production facilities geared to export, produces a sort of resource export trap where in order to pay for foreign investment Canada has to export, and in order to export, Canada has to invest in capital-intensive infrastructure, which can only be paid for through additional exports. In the meantime investment in facilities to serve Canadian markets is neglected, in part because of the constant pressure to export and in part because foreign investors are guided by strategies developed abroad. Foreign-owned resource companies exist to serve head offices at home, not Canada.

The historical experience of Canadian economic development teaches us that in bad times foreign investors still expect, and are often in a position to demand, a good return on their money. While the bishops criticize Canada's reliance on foreign ownership, the business community, generally supported by Canadian governments, wants more foreign investments. Yet export revenues may be insufficient to pay for both the cost of servicing foreign loans and the operating expenses of the domestic infrastructure needed to promote exports. At this point it becomes clear that domestic costs have to be subsidized unless one is prepared to alienate foreign investors.

This subsidization may be collective; for instance, the deficit of the Canadian National Railways is ultimately covered through tax revenue. It may be the case that workers are asked to directly absorb the cost of the subsidy through wage restraint. But what should be clear is that the decisions made to orientate Canadian production towards export markets concern all Canadians. Yet do Canadians have a voice in these policy decisions? Are they consulted about investment expenditures?

The short answer is that in the case of public policy decisions, Canadians have an indirect voice through elected representatives. In the case of private investment decisions, the amount of input by either the general public or elected officials is usually minimal. However, ultimately Canadians are directly affected by private investment decisions, and collectively, through governments, they absorb a portion of the costs. This is clearest when a major company like Dome Petroleum gets into difficulty, but it is also the case that most business couldn't operate without services provided by governments.

It is this aspect of economic policy that concerns the bishops: workers and their communities share the burdens of economic growth, but mechanisms for assuming the responsibility for economic matters largely escape local and regional control. And the benefits of economic growth are distributed unequally. This assessment leads the bishops to propose the alternative of self-sufficient, community-controlled development.

The alternative perspective provided by the bishops has been poorly received by the business community. Some suggest that the bishops want to return to an earlier, less complicated world; others question the viability of self-reliance as an economic policy. But what the bishops suggest is that criteria on which we judge economic projects—principally profitability—seem to lead to a future where capital and energy-intensive production displaces jobs, and an export orientation and foreign investment neglect Canadian priorities. The bishops propose that additional criteria be applied to economic policy. Does investment meet human needs? Are jobs being created? Are wealth and power being distributed equitably?

Rather than seeing the ability to conquer overseas markets and increase profits as the ultimate tests of economic viability, the New Year's Statement argues for an alternative to corporate economics. Among its features would be community ownership and control of industries, worker management and ownership, and socially useful production using appropriate technologies and renewable energy sources. Does this represent pie-in-the-sky fantasy?

Obviously, for those who find the dominant economic model satisfactory, there is no need to envisage alternative futures. If our present economic system represents the best we can do, any policies which question it are wrong-headed by definition. For the bishops, and one suspects for many other Canadians as well, something is amiss in our society, seriously amiss; and the question of what shape our society should take in the future is worth examining. From this perspective there are two aspects to a discussion of the economic future: what goals should be favoured? And how should we proceed—what means should be employed to reach our goals?

The New Year's Statement encourages debate and discussion that would integrate the consideration of means and ends. In a sense, the report seems to be saying that the means adopted within a society determine the character of the society and become its ends. As a result, the bishops embrace the democratic ideal that communities must control their destiny. This is the meaning of the self-reliant development alternative. In a real way, such a proposal precludes the presentation of a blueprint for economic development by the bishops. An authoritative design for the future would be in contradiction with the very idea that communities must themselves work together to decide upon and create their own future. But consideration of the alternatives offered for discussion by the report is instructive.

One major result of the recession has been that enterprises have been closing plants, shutting down operating divisions and generally scaling down production. Instead of simply leaving factories empty, some corporations have been prepared to sell off productive facilities. Among the potential purchasers are of course the principal interested parties: local government, employees and communities directly affected by closures. And some employee buyouts have taken place.

Canada does not yet have in place comprehensive legislation requiring that companies justify their actions when they eliminate jobs and, in some instances, entire communities through layoffs and closures. But industrial shutdowns are a common feature of our troubled times. Canadian practice favours the rights of property owners to dispose of their assets without providing for public accountability. This differs from European practice where companies are required to meet legislative criteria, including consultation with labour unions, before closing production facilities. An immediate consequence of this type of legislation is that firms are inclined to take a long view of the costs involved in both setting up plants and in closing them.[31] This means that workers are viewed more as partners than is the case in Canada. In some European countries, legislation requires that workers be represented on the board of directors of companies, and it is interesting to note that the Commission of the European Community has proposed that this be required of foreign-owned TNCs as well. (Canadian TNCs have objected to this proposal and have lobbied against it in Brussels.)

The bishops' concern that manufacturing industry be strengthened surely implies that public authorities look much more closely at the effects of company decisions to "dis-invest." Not only should more information and justification be required from companies, but resources and support should be available for local, community and employee takeovers of assets. This is one means of implementing the self-reliance alternative. Rather than depend upon foreign investors, public policy should be oriented towards replacing the sort of support networks TNCs are able to provide.

The rather limited experience of employee-owned and -operated enterprise in Canada does not provide as yet a basis for judging the viability of this particular alternative.[32] But that these operations are able to go ahead without a coherent public policy framework to support them does attest to willingness by some groups to explore this alternative to economic dislocation. The new directions the bishops propose for discussion in fact depend on "the aspirations and skills of working men and women [which are] required to build an alternative economic future." The message of the New Year's Statement is that Canadians, and citizens of other countries, must look first to themselves if they wish to build a true community and a new economic order.

Conclusion: The Political Agenda

An economic future that would combine human labour and economic resources to provide for basic needs within a framework of local, worker and community control means establishing an alternative form of economic power. This is a political task and not a religious or scientific matter. This explains why neither a bishop nor a political economist can provide the means for implementing a new economic order. But the bishops have issued a challenge to Canadians to rethink the present. Significantly, they have taken a stand themselves. In this book, my colleague Gregory Baum examines Catholic thought in Canada and abroad in order to assess the theological and social reasoning that led to the New Year's Statement. His analysis provides us with an understanding of the nature of the bishops' commitment to economic justice. What remains an open question is the willingness of Canadians to meet the challenge "to envision and develop alternatives to the dominant economic model that governs our society."

Government economic strategies require political support. When prominent business leaders call for public sector wage restraint, when the anti-inflation messages of the financial community are echoed in the press, and when economic summit meetings lead to the adoption of consensus views among Western leaders about the importance of wages in the inflationary spiral, the policies of government, whatever the nominal party label, are unlikely to diverge from these dominant views.

In order to promote alternative economic strategies, political support from other sources is necessary, and this has been recognized by Bishop Remi de Roo, chair of the Social Affairs Commission. In an article commenting on the reactions to the New Year's Statement, he points out that a social movement committed to economic justice is necessary if policy changes are to be brought about.[33] The bishops' opposition to government policies can then be understood as an indication of the terms on which the continuing struggle for public opinion are to be waged: those who favour anti-inflationary policies, such as monetarism and wage restraint on the one side, and those who favour full employment and industrial strategies on the other side.

The bishops advance an alternative explanation of the current economic crisis. Let there be no mistake about it: their argument is an appeal to the dispossessed. It seeks to offer to those with little stake in society an alternative to welfare and unemployment. But the argument is also an invitation to those who may feel powerless to take charge of their interests as workers. The New Year's Statement is an attack on orthodoxy and official opinion, from the point of view of Christian thought, of course, but also from the perspective of entering into a confrontation with forces that would exercise influence over the future course of our society.

The New Year's Statement notes that in some communities and regions Christian groups have joined with others in activities and events that promote economic justice. The bishops encourage them to continue doing so. Specifically the report suggests that forums could be organized "to discuss: (a) specific struggles of workers, the poor and the unemployed in local communities; (b) analysis of local and regional economic problems and structures; (c) major ethical principles of economic life in the Church's recent social teachings; (d) suggestions for alternative economic visions; (e) new proposals for industrial strategies that reflect basic ethical principles."

For concrete social and economic change to come about, the democratic ideals and concern for each individual life that are expressed by the bishops must become a part of daily existence in all spheres of society—but especially in the workplaces that make up the economy. If people are to exercise control over their lives, it can only come through the recognition that rights to profit and to proceeds of private property are not some sort of economic law derived from scientific understanding.

Rather such rights, which have become the pre-eminent principles of economic organization, are politically founded, and they can be modified, restrained or changed through political action—that is, by building democratic support for alternative conceptions of relations among members of society. For the bishops, the ethical principles of Christianity cannot be set aside when examining economic life. Political democracy requires that economic assumptions and practices be given the open discussion and examination the bishops have called for and the New Year's Statement has received. "Ethical Reflections" rejects the view that politics can be restricted to technical discussion of issues by experts. They judge decision-making processes not by their conformity with professional or bureaucratic rationality but rather by their contribution to advancement of human values.[34] Are decisions rooted in local communities? Do they reflect social priorities?

In this respect, the bishops join with those who have long questioned dominant modes of thinking, enquiry and action. Their political vision is not separate from many social practices that have evolved in Canada and elsewhere as part of the struggle for a better life. Like social critics of any age, Canada's Roman Catholic bishops have been vilified by some; but unlike most messages of dissent from consensus views, their statement has been honoured by the attention it has received from friends and foes alike. Herein lies its political importance.

Appendix 1*

Northern Development: At What Cost?

Labour Day Message, 1975
Canadian Catholic Conference

Introduction

1. A cry for justice rings out today from Native Peoples who inhabit the Canadian North. Dramatically, on a massive scale the Native Peoples of the North find themselves and their way of life being threatened by the headlong search for new energy sources on this continent.

2. At the same time, other voices are raising serious ethical questions about the enormous demands for energy required to maintain high standards of wealth and comfort in industrial society. A variety of public interest groups are calling for greater care of the environment and responsible stewardship of the energy resources in this country.

3. We, Catholic bishops of Canada, want to echo these cries for justice and demands for stewardship in the Canadian North. They tell us much about ourselves as citizens and consumers, the industrial society of North

---

*Editor's note: Each appendix is reprinted exactly as in the original statement, except for minor changes made for stylistic consistency.

America, and the Native Peoples of the North. As Christians, we cannot ignore the pressing ethical issues of northern development. For the living God, the God we worship, is the Lord of Creation and Justice.

4. We wish to share with you, fellow citizens, some reflections and judgments on the ethical problems posed by the industrial development of the Canadian North.[1] We hope that these reflections and judgments will contribute to more public debate and stimulate alternative policies regarding the future development of the North. We also ask that these expressed concerns be tested in the public arena along with other points of view.

The Northern Dilemma

5. Since "time beyond memory," the vast land mass that covers the northern tips of our provinces and the sub-Arctic regions has been the home for many of this country's Native Peoples, the Indians, Inuit and Métis. Through time, these Native Peoples developed social, cultural, economic and religious patterns of life which were in harmony with the rhythms of the land itself.[2]

6. This land has been the source of livelihood for a significant portion of northern Native Peoples, along with a number of early white settlers. It has been the basis of their traditional economy of hunting, fishing and trapping. For the Native Peoples the land is more than simply a source of food or cash. The land itself constitutes a permanent sense of security, well-being and identity. For generations, this land has defined the basis of what the natives are as a people. In their own words, "Our land is our life."[3]

7. After countless generations of occupation, use and care, the Native Peoples of the North have come to claim their rights to these lands.[4] While some northern natives are giving up their life of hunting, fishing and trapping, these lands remain essential to their future economic development. For these northern lands contain a natural storehouse of some of the most valuable resources on this continent: potential reserves of oil and gas, powerful river systems and rich mineral deposits.

8. But now the "energy crisis" in the industrial world is posing a serious challenge to the people and resources of the northern lands. The search for new supplies of oil, gas and electricity on this continent is largely focused on the untapped energy resources of the Canadian North.

9. In recent years, provincial governments, crown corporations and private companies have been planning large-scale projects to harness the power potential of the northern rivers. Dams, power plants, railroads and highways are now under construction in several provinces:

- the James Bay hydro project in northern Quebec;
- the Churchill-Nelson hydro development in northern Manitoba;
- the Churchill Falls hydro project in Labrador; and
- the hydroelectric plants in northwest British Columbia.

10. Simultaneously, the Canadian North has been cited as a major region for potential reserves of oil and gas. Assisted by the federal government, the giants of the oil industry—Exxon, Shell, Gulf, Mobil, Sunoco and others—have led the way, through their Canadian subsidiaries, in making discoveries and initiating plans to build several major industrial projects:[5]

- the Mackenzie Valley pipeline in the Northwest Territories to bring natural gas from Alaska and the Canadian Arctic to southern Canada and the United States;
- the Polar Gas pipeline designed to bring natural gas from the high Arctic to the Maritimes and the United States;
- the Syncrude project to develop the Athabaska tarsands in northern Alberta.

11. In this way the Canadian North is fast becoming a centre stage in a continental struggle to gain control of new energy sources. The critical issue is *how* these northern energy resources are to be developed—by whom and for whom. We are especially concerned that the future of the North not be determined by colonial patterns of development, wherein a powerful few end up controlling both the people and the resources.

12. Some present examples of industrial planning give us cause for grave concern.[6] For what we see emerging in the Canadian North are forms of exploitation which we often assume happen only in Third World countries: a serious abuse of both the Native Peoples and the energy resources of the North.[7] Herein lies the northern dilemma. What has been described as the "last frontier" in the building of this nation may become our own "Third World."

Demands for Justice

13. Our first pastoral concern is that justice be done in the future industrial development of the Canadian North. In various parts of the northern lands the Native Peoples' protests have drawn attention to a series of injustices:

- In several cases, governments and corporations have secretly planned and suddenly announced the construction of large industrial projects without prior consultation with the people who will be most directly affected.[8] As a result the future lives of these Native Peoples and their communities tend to be planned *for* them by southern interests.
- The plans for these industrial projects are usually finalized and implemented *before* land-claim settlements have been reached with the Native People of the region.[9] Yet, for people whose land is their life, and who wish to secure control over their future economic development, a just settlement of their land claims lies at the very heart of their struggle for justice.

- The construction of these industrial projects has sometimes proceeded without an adequate assessment of their environmental and social consequences. In several instances, the building of power plants and hydro dams will cause the flooding of vast areas of land, damage to the vegetation and wildlife, and the relocation of whole communities of people whose lives have traditionally depended on hunting, fishing and trapping.[10]
- The promise of jobs in the construction of these industrial projects has offered no real alternative way of life. For most of the Native Peoples, these jobs are temporary, paying relatively low wages for low-skilled labour.[11]

14. As a result, more and more Native People are being compelled to give up their land-based economy and move into the urban centres where alcoholism and welfarism have become prevalent for many. While compensation may be offered, money can hardly replace the loss of land and what it means to the lives of the Native Peoples and their future economic development.

15. A sense of justice, coming from the living God, tells us there are better ways of developing the resources of the Canadian North. The Lord of Creation has given mankind the responsibility to develop the resources of Nature so as to make possible a fuller human life for all peoples.[12] This coincides with the beliefs of the Native Peoples who have traditionally called for a "communal sharing" of the land which belongs to the Creator.

16. To develop the resources of the Canadian North is a responsibility to be shared by all who live in this country—North and South. While Native Peoples of the North must be prepared to share in this responsibility, they rightly demand that their claims to justice be realized. In the words of one northern native leader:

> We also want to participate in Canadian society, but we want to participate as equals. It is impossible

> to be equal if our economic development is subordinated to the profit-oriented priorities of the American multinationals . . . . the Native People are saying we must have a large degree of control over our own economic development. Without control we will end up like our brothers and sisters on the reserves in the South: continually powerless, threatened and impoverished.[13]

17. Across the Canadian North, Native Peoples' groups have begun to articulate a common program for justice.[14] Their goal is greater control over their own economic development. The key is a just settlement of their land claims. In recent years, native groups have been taking the land issue into the courtrooms to establish their traditional rights to these lands.

18. The living God calls on us to respond to these demands for justice. Christian love of neighbour and justice cannot be separated in the development of people. "For love implies an absolute demand for justice, namely a recognition of the dignity and rights of one's neighbour."[15]

Demands for Stewardship

19. A second pastoral concern is the demand for responsible stewardship of energy resources in the development of the Canadian North. Throughout this country, public interest groups are raising serious questions about our highly industrialized society and the current exploitation of northern energy resources.

- The scramble for northern energy continues without adequate measures to regulate the patterns of relentless consumption in this country. In the last twenty-five years alone, Canada's consumption of oil, gas and electricity has multiplied three times over.[16] This extravagant consumption of energy generates increasing demands for the rapid development of northern resources.

- Northern development is also continuing without full public discussion of future energy needs. Governments and industries predict that Canada's energy needs will have to multiply four more times by the end of this century to maintain "a high quality of life."[17] But what is this "quality of life" and who determines what these future energy needs should be?
- The reasons for rapidly developing northern energy resources on such a massive scale at this time have also been seriously questioned.[18] While the sale of these resources will reap large profits for the energy industry now, it may also cause the rapid depletion of non-renewable supplies of oil and gas required for the future.
- In several cases, this energy is being rapidly developed now to feed the industrial centres of the United States.[19] Yet, there are many other countries, especially poor nations of the Third World, that are suffering from acute shortages of energy required for basic survival.

20. The United States and Canada are ranked as the highest users of energy in the world today. For these two countries, containing little more than 6.5 per cent of the world's population, consume about 43 per cent of the energy supplies of this planet.[20] All this energy goes to run the countless number of machines which have become "our energy slaves" in industries, businesses and homes. It is now estimated that given the amount of muscular power required to do the work of these machines, each North American has the equivalent of 400 "energy slaves" working for him.[21]

21. We North Americans have created a highly industrialized society that places exorbitant demands on limited supplies of energy. The maximization of consumption, profit and power has become the operating principle of this society. These are the driving forces behind the present continental struggle to gain control of northern energy resources.[22] These are the idols which turn many from service of man and world, and, thus, from the living God.

22. As a culture, we have not faced up to the fact that the world God created has its limits. Many voices now warn that mankind has reached a "turning point" in history: crucial decisions must be made now to stop plundering the Earth's non-renewable resources before it is too late.[23] Yet, this industrialized society treats the resources of the Earth as if they were limitless.

23. In recent years, public interest groups have been calling for responsible stewardship of northern energy resources. They are calling for more effective measures to reduce levels of consumption and waste and preserve non-renewable resources. These groups contend that future resource development, which is largely controlled today by multinational corporations, must be made more accountable to the Canadian public.

24. The living God calls us to a life of caring, sparing, sharing the limited resources of this planet.[24] This is no longer simply a moral imperative. It has also become a practical necessity for the survival of our common humanity.[25]

Northern Alternatives

25. We readily acknowledge that the Catholic Church must also take a critical look at itself. We now see that, coming from another culture, the Church may have contributed to disruptive changes in native culture while helping to bring Christianity to the North through the creative efforts of missionaries who have shared the hard lives of the people. At the same time, the Church has participated with others in the wealth and comfort of an industrial society which places enormous demands on energy resources at the expense of other people.

26. We look to the past in order that we may learn to act more responsibly in the present. The present industrial development of the Canadian North poses new challenges for the Church. Some of our northern dioceses have been re-evaluating their missionary work in the light of these challenges.[26] But the responsibility lies with *all* of us who comprise the Church in Canada.

27. We believe that the Spirit is challenging the whole Church to fulfill its prophetic service in society today. As the Third Synod of Bishops asserted in 1971: "Action on behalf of justice and participation in the transformation of the world fully appear to us as a constitutive dimension of the preaching of the Gospel, or, in other words, of the Church's mission for the redemption of the human race and its liberation from every oppressive situation."[27]

28. We contend, therefore, that there are better ways of developing the Canadian North. What is required today is a public search for alternative policies for northern development. This search is already under way through the activities of Native Peoples and public interest groups across the country.[28]

29. We find ourselves in solidarity with many of these initiatives. Based on the ethical principles of social justice and responsible stewardship, we believe that the following conditions must be met *before* any final decisions are made to proceed with specific projects for northern development:

- sufficient public discussion and debate about proposed industrial projects, based on independent studies of energy needs and social costs of the proposed developments;
- achievement of a just land settlement with the Native Peoples, including hunting, fishing and trapping rights and fair royalties in return for the extraction of valuable resources from their land claims;
- effective participation by the Native Peoples in shaping the kind of regional development, beginning with effective control over their own future economic development;

- adequate measures to protect the terrain, vegetation, wildlife and waters of northern areas, based on complete and independent studies of the regional environment to be affected by proposed developments; and
- adequate controls to regulate the extraction of energy resources from the North, to prevent the rapid depletion of oil, gas and other resources which are non-renewable.

30. It remains to be seen whether Canada's "last frontier" will be developed according to the principles of justice and stewardship. The next two years will be a crucial testing period. In some cases, final and irreversible decisions have already been made. In other instances, there may still be a chance to alter the course of development. The Mackenzie Valley pipeline proposals presently being reviewed by the Berger Commission and the National Energy Board could provide the real test.
31. As Christians, as citizens, we have a responsibility to insist that the future development of the Canadian North be based on social justice and responsible stewardship. As responsible citizens are *we* prepared to:

- study one or more of the industrial projects in the northern parts of our provinces or the Territories?
- actively support Native Peoples' organizations and public interest groups currently striving to change the policies of northern development?
- engage policy makers, both federal and provincial, and local members of Parliament in a public dialogue about the ethical issues of northern development?
- raise ethical questions about corporations involved in northern development, especially those corporations in which Church institutions may have shares?
- seek a just settlement regarding specific Church landholdings that are subject to native claims?
- design education programs to examine personal lifestyles and change the patterns of wasteful energy

consumption in our homes, churches, schools and places of work?
- collaborate with the other Canadian churches, in every way possible, in a common Christian effort to achieve the above objectives?

32. In the final analysis what is required is nothing less than fundamental social change. Until we as a society begin to change our own lifestyles based on wealth and comfort, until we begin to change the profit-oriented priorities of our industrial system, we will continue placing exorbitant demands on the limited supplies of energy in the North and end up exploiting the people of the North in order to get those resources.

Conclusion

33. We wish to emphasize that this message is only one step in the continuing struggle for justice and stewardship in the Canadian North. For our part, we want to join with other members of the Catholic community, fellow Christians, members of the other faiths, and fellow citizens. Together, we may be able to act in solidarity with the Native Peoples of the North, in a common search for more creative ways of developing the "last frontier" of this country.

34. Ultimately, the challenge before us is a test of our faithfulness in the living God. For we believe that the struggle for justice and responsible stewardship in the North today, like that in distant Third World countries, is the voice of the Lord among us. We are called to involve ourselves in these struggles, to become active at the very centre of human history where the great voice of God cries out for the fullness of life.

Appendix 2

From Words to Action

Canadian Catholic Conference
Labour Day Message, 1976

Urgent Signs of the Times

1. The signs of the times today compel us as Christians to think about our social responsibilities and to put our words into action. We live in a world that oppresses at least half the human race and this scandal threatens to get worse.[1] Right around us, human suffering of many kinds scars the face of Canada: poverty for many, inflating prices, housing crises, regional disparities, strikes and lockouts, cultural violations, native land claims, overcrowded cities and rural neglect. With all this comes a growing sense of loneliness, powerlessness and alienation in our society and institutions.[2] So we have cause for deep concern. But it is not enough to see injustice, disorder and violence at home and abroad and to worry about the future. These conditions will not improve on their own. We, the people, have the responsibility to change them.

What Gospel Response?

2. As Christians, we are faced with the question: What does faith in Jesus Christ tell us about our social and political responsibilities in these times? This is the basic question that we, as pastors of the Catholic Church in Canada, wish to address in this message to our brothers and sisters in the Catholic community. Some will say that this is an old question and so it is. We have talked about some aspect of it in every one of our Labour Day statements and pastoral messages.[3] Now more than ever there is urgent need to bring the following questions to the centre of our daily lives: What does the Gospel say about the creation of a new social order based on justice? What should a follower of Christ do in response to the many struggles for social justice going on around us?

A New Social Order

3. Many people agree that there is something wrong with the present social and economic order. It fails to meet the human needs of the majority of people. The present economic order results in the very uneven distribution of wealth and the control of resources by a small minority. On the global scene, the poor peoples, especially in the Third World, are calling for the creation of a new economic order based on a just distribution of wealth and power. And within this country, in its various regions and communities, there are similar signs that people want to find new approaches now, to make better use of human and material resources, to end waste and want and exploitation.[4]

Gospel Message of Justice

4. As disciples of Christ, all of us have a responsibility to play a role in the creation of a social order based on justice. For we stand in the biblical tradition of the prophets of Israel where to know God is to seek justice for the disinherited, the poor and the oppressed (Amos, Jeremiah, Isaiah). The same Spirit of God that came upon the prophets filled Jesus of Nazareth. With the power of that Spirit, Jesus prayed and healed, all the while proclaiming that the Kingdom of God was at hand (Matthew 4:17, 23; Luke 6:12, 11:1-4). In the light of the Spirit he announced he was the message of the prophets come true—"the good news to the poor" and "liberty to the oppressed" (Luke 4:18, 19).

True Liberation

5. For the Christian community this struggle for justice is not an optional activity. It is integral to bringing the Gospel to the world.[5] True, God's Kingdom and hence the mission of the Church reach far beyond this world (John 18:36). This mission goes further than mere liberation in the economic, political, social and cultural ordering of our lives. True liberation encompasses the whole person and makes men and women open to God.[6] This openness allows us to see the limits of our human activity and forces us to search for greater liberation. Yet, this dimension of our religious life can be no excuse for retreating from the affairs of this world. Rather, it calls us to work even harder for the creation of a just social order.

We Judge by the Gospel

6. The Gospel, today as always, gives us a basis for judging the social order that is the product of human activity.[7] In that light we have focused our attention in recent years on the development of the earth's resources to meet the needs of people.[8] We have urged the heads of government and corporations to assure that the earth's resources be developed not for the profits of a few but to serve the basic needs of the majority of people in this country and the world.[9] Who shall control and who shall benefit from the earth's natural resources? Will these resources be used to enrich a small minority? Or will they be developed to meet the unfulfilled needs of the majority of mankind for adequate food, shelter, health care, education and employment for a fuller human life?[10]

A Significant Minority

7. Across Canada today, there are some encouraging signs among Christian people who are raising these and related ethical questions. Much of this activity for social justice and responsible stewardship of resources is occurring on an ecumenical basis. A variety of Christian groups have been working with the poor and oppressed peoples of their communities, organizing educational events on issues of injustice, and pressing leaders of governments and industries to change policies that cause human suffering. Unfortunately, those who are committed to this Christian way of life are presently a minority in the life of the Catholic community. Yet, this minority is significant because it is challenging the whole Church to live the gospel message by serving the needs of the people.

Called to Conversion

8. As pastoral leaders, we have a responsibility to see that every member of the Church becomes fully alive in the service of God and neighbour. In this light, we would like to see more members of the Catholic community commit their lives to the task of creating a more just social order. But what does this really mean for us as persons? Clearly, the Gospel calls us to become new men and women in the service of others.[11] It also calls us to a conversion of attitudes leading to a change of those structures that cause human suffering. And this conversion requires all of us to see the reality of everyday life in a new light: from the perspective of Jesus Christ and his concern for the poor and the oppressed.

9. We propose the following six guidelines to help each of us—bishops, priests, religious and laity—commit ourselves more deeply to this new way of life as disciples of Christ.

- *Understanding the true meaning of the gospel message of Justice.* Clearly, some among us have never understood or [have] lost sight of this gospel message of love *and* justice or the social teachings of the Church. What is the relation between our personal and collective faith in Jesus Christ and the demands for social justice? Jesus taught that Christian love of neighbour means, first and foremost, identification with the plight of the poor and the oppressed. We must find relevant ways of probing the true meaning of this gospel message. This calls for communities of people reflecting and acting on specific injustices in the light of the Gospel. Our community and religious education programs should give greater attention to these concerns.
- *Modifying our more affluent lifestyles.* We live in a society where people are encouraged to consume and waste extravagantly while others are left wanting. As Christians, we are called to turn away from self-seeking and material treasures (Luke 12:33-34). The teaching that "man does not live by bread alone" (Deuteronomy 8:3) is meant, among other things, to direct the more affluent away from this consumer way of life. Modifying luxurious living habits will not, itself, overcome the gross disparities and inequities among people today. But it can renew our spirit and open our hearts to the plight of the poor in our midst.
- *Listening to the victims of injustice in our own communities.* Most of us have had little experience with the human suffering of poverty and oppression. Jesus taught that we can learn a great deal about justice from those who have suffered under these conditions (Matthew 25:31-46). We can achieve a new vision of reality by becoming more present with the hungry, the homeless, the jobless, the native person, the poor

immigrant and others who may be victims of injustices in our communities. By listening to their problems and sharing in their struggle, we can learn much more about the attitudes, activities and structures that cause human suffering and what can be done about them.

- *Speaking out against the injustices in our communities.* Too often, people see examples of exploitation around them but remain silent. Yet, silence amounts to a form of consent and approval of what is happening. In the tradition of the prophets, we are called to denounce injustice and speak the truth to those in power. As citizens we must exercise our freedom and responsibility to take positions on specific issues and speak out against the causes of injustice. Until the voices for justice are multiplied, they will continue to be ignored by those who hold power.
- *Participating in actions to change the causes of injustice.* It is not enough to denounce social ills and talk about a new order. Social justice is the goal. Political action is a means to obtain that goal. We are called to participate in actions to change the policies of governments, corporations and other institutions that cause human suffering. People must come together to act for fundamental social change. This is our political responsibility as Christians and citizens in a democratic society.[12] We can exercise this responsibility by participating in religious and community groups acting today on specific examples of injustice.
- *Providing assistance to poor and oppressed groups.* The people experiencing poverty and oppression have a primary role to play in bringing about a more just social order. But many of these people and their groups remain powerless. As Christians, we have a responsibility not simply to feed the hungry but to increase their power to change the causes of hunger. Some church groups are now providing funds, technical assistance and other forms of communal support to poverty groups involved in social change. This frater-

nal activity can help to increase effectiveness in action and offset frustrations which may lead to violence. Yet, much more could be done.

Disturbing Experience

10. The challenge of living the Gospel of justice in this way is a disturbing experience for all of us. Some who have committed themselves to this new way of life have been misunderstood and criticized, particularly by the more affluent and powerful sectors of their communities. Yet, the message of Christ crucified is not a comforting message. We cannot take refuge in the position that, as Christians, our duty is simply to worship God and give alms to the poor (Matthew 7:21-23). To do this alone in our present situation would be to incur the wrath of Christ because, like the Pharisees, we would be neglecting "justice and the love of God" (Luke 11:42).

Invitation to All

11. We urge all our brothers and sisters to join us in a continuing process of acting and reflecting on these pastoral guidelines. It is in our local communities that we can best exercise these social and political responsibilities. This calls for our personal and collective participation in local struggles for justice with the jobless, exploited workers, poor or lonely immigrants, small producers, native people, culturally oppressed peoples and others. We therefore ask local Christian communities to stimulate and intensify this kind of activity through special study/action projects as well as existing family and religious education programs. And we urge leaders in the political and economic spheres of Canada to increase their efforts towards the building of a more just social order. Such actions will say, louder than any words: "I am in the midst of you as one who serves" (Luke 22:27).

Sign of Hope

12. In a world being torn apart by injustice and conflict, this kind of active Christian witness will be a sign of hope. It both illustrates and contributes to the building of the Kingdom of God. For His Kingdom is an expression of the power of love, service and self-giving, to all in need. This requires personal and collective prayer combined with vital public action. We must always remember that the credibility, authenticity, and acceptance of our worship is conditioned by the exercise of justice (Matthew 5:23-24). Only then will we be an authentic Christian community praising God through our actions as well as our words.

Appendix 3

A Society to Be Transformed

A Pastoral Message by the Catholic Bishops of Canada, December 1, 1977

1. Even though our times are scarred by grave social ills, a number of Christians find reasons for hope. In many parts of the country, members of Christian communities are coming to know God more deeply by their efforts to overcome human sufferings. As they join in struggles for justice, especially for the poor and oppressed, Christians find other groups striving to reach the same goal. All such social efforts against poverty and other forms of injustice and inequality are truly sources of hope.

2. We must not be misled, however, if there are some good efforts and a few gains. We live in a world simmering with uncertainty, contradictions and conflicts. Everywhere, people express their concern about the future. By comparison with many others, our own country seems particularly prosperous and peaceful. Nevertheless, we are reminded every day that we too have imbalances and tensions, violence and fears of violence.

Signs of Underdevelopment

3. Although our country is called developed, it has many marks of underdevelopment. In 1971 one person in four had an income below the poverty level.[1] Since then, inflation and high unemployment rates have worsened the situation. Powerful foreign-controlled companies exercise increasing power in society beyond the reach of effective public intervention. Their decisions directly influence housing, unemployment, increasing prices and the declining value of earnings and savings. Economic and social disparities between regions of the country persist. Pollution and other forms of environmental damage show that natural resources are misused. Entire groups who are central to our country's future are uncertain of the survival of their very culture and customs. Workers, even those in unions, have little share in decisions affecting their livelihood and well-being. In turn, elected representatives at various levels of government seem to face insurmountable difficulties.

4. It could be said that this situation is not new. Indeed, in a series of statements extending back more than twenty years, we, the Roman Catholic bishops of Canada, have spoken frequently about these and other ills of our society. However, people are more conscious today of the social malaise. Every day the news media report protests today about actual conditions or new proposals for changing them. The diversity of these proposals shows that we face contradictory values and many views of mankind and of the world.

Two-fold Purpose

5. We speak again about these matters to you, the Catholics of Canada, for two reasons. We invite you to get more involved in reshaping society, and we urge a particular form of involvement. First, in the name of the Gospel, all Christians must involve themselves in transforming our ways of living and our social and economic structures. The Lord calls Christians to be present in every search for new or renewed ways—new or renewed techniques, plans, programs, institutions or systems—to resolve today's difficulties. Secondly, we stress once again that Christians must be leaders in identifying and promoting the solutions that come only through new or renewed values, attitudes and relationships.

6. At any period, ideas rule the world. People are guided by the values carried by current ideologies. For our part, we find in the Scriptures a concept of justice which lights the way for today. People will see their rights and needs respected and satisfied to the extent that men and women relate to one another in terms of justice and equality, and work together to shape institutions and structures according to these values.

Reasons for Hope

7. The difficulties we face are, for you and for us, a time and a place for making the incarnation and redemption of Christ ever more real in today's world:

> The Christian's hope comes primarily from the fact that he knows that the Lord is working with us in the world, continuing in His Body which is the Church—and, through the Church, in the whole of mankind—the Redemption which was accomplished on the cross and which burst forth in victory on the morning of the resurrection. This hope springs also from the fact that the Christian knows that other men are at work, to undertake actions of justice and peace working for the same ends.[2]

Christian Calling

8. The world in which we live recalls both Nineveh, the city of sin and pride, and Jerusalem, the Holy City, the place where God is encountered.[3] Work in such a world has special meaning for Christians. We have, as Pope Paul VI has said, "the mission of sharing in the creation of the supernatural world which remains incomplete until we all come to build up together that perfect man of whom St. Paul speaks 'who realizes the fullness of Christ.' "[4] Expectation of that new earth stimulates our concern for cultivating this one, "for here grows the body of a new human family, a body which even now is able to give some kind of foreshadowing of the new age."[5] God's Kingdom is still to come and yet has begun.[6]

9. All Christians, poor, rich and in between, are called to "put on the new self" and "be reconciled to God."[7] This two-fold call comes from God who created the world and intervenes in human history as our Father, champion of love and justice. His love extends to all; in a special way he is the friend of the lowly, the outcast, those oppressed by any evil. By his word we are called to turn from self-seeking and greed, to respect and care for one another, to love our neighbour as ourself.

10. A central theme running through the Scriptures is that we come to know God, to experience him truly, by loving and respecting others in seeking justice for the poor, the disinherited, the oppressed, the aged, sick and imprisoned.[8] This love requires that we fully respect the rights of others, renounce any will to dominate, and establish the truest possible justice in all our relationships. The foundation of this true respect is the love that God has for everyone without exception. God is love. In Christ the Father loves all of us so that we may love one another, a love that is the new commandment.[9] Indeed, if we do not love other people whom we can see, we cannot love God whom we cannot see.[10] This kind of love leads on to a justice that seeks to promote greater equality among people.[11]

11. On Mount Sinai, God joined with his people in a Covenant that was renewed in the death and resurrection of Jesus Christ. Inheritors of that Covenant, Christians have received the mission to reunite all people with God by undertaking, as an ongoing challenge, the building of a kingdom based on justice and love. By the grace of baptism, we are remade in the image of God and plunged into a new life. Our participation in the Eucharist announces the glory that is to come and introduces us, even now, to the kingdom that the Father has promised us. To these gifts of God we must reply by endless conversion, reconciliation and penance. Thus we place ourselves under the law of Christ[12] and keep the Covenant with Him. The spirit of the Beatitudes challenges Christians to transform the world in the name of Jesus. It inspires us to become peacemakers, merciful, pure in heart, poor in spirit, hungry and thirsty for justice, even when afflicted and persecuted.[13]

Discerning the Gospel's Message

12. God wills that the Gospel should transform not just our personal and private life but also all social and public behaviour, that is, the attitudes, customs, laws and structures of the world in which we live.[14] He calls on us to build a more humane and fraternal world, in which injustice and violence no longer threaten, where no one person fears another, and where the resources of his creation are developed to supply what all people need for a decent life. It is up to Christian communities, Pope Paul VI has emphasized, "to analyze with objectivity the situation which is proper to their own country, to shed on it the light of the Gospel's unalterable words and to draw principles of reflection, norms of judgment and directives for action from the social teachings of the Church."[15] Applying the Gospel in this way to our own times, we are better able to identify and evaluate what is going on around us and make a positive contribution to human development.

Heritage of Capitalism

13. Some of the achievements of modern industrial society have been real factors in human progress. The secrets of nature are being gradually revealed through systematic research and much hard work. People have learned how to organize vast and daring ventures that could make the earth's riches available to all. However, despite the place given to individual freedoms, this potential remains largely unrealized. Instead, a woeful system has been constructed on the new conditions of society, a system "which considers profit as the key motive for economic progress, competition as the supreme law of economics, and private ownership of the means of production as an absolute right that has no limits and carries no corresponding social obligation."[16] With no vision of an afterlife, this world is pictured solely as a place where people struggle for an ever more comfortable existence. The single-minded pursuit of self-interest is presented as a value. The theory of the survival of the fittest leads many to accept widespread poverty and the concentration of wealth and power in the hands of a few. Industrial strategies are designed specifically to produce maximum gratification and profit, so that wasteful consumption is systematically promoted. In the process, both human beings and natural resources are abused or destroyed.

14. In many ways, our country is still profoundly marked by the founders of liberal capitalism. We carry forward many of the consequences of their lives, for their ideas have become our institutions. Their values shape much of today's economic system which, in turn, gives rise to materialistic aspirations that are the idols that millions worship today. Those values constitute an economic religion that inhibits the development of an ethic of sharing. While people have worked hard to plant the seeds of human solidarity and love, the dominant economic and social structures of our times have become the rocky ground of self-service and self-aggrandizement. The result is clear: many are kept from achieving certain basic necessities while others, trapped in their wealth, find great difficulty in meeting God, in knowing the person of Jesus and living his message. Succeeding generations are drawn into a culture, into ways of thinking and behaving, alien to God's purpose.

Marxist Alternative

15. A growing number of our fellow citizens can no longer accept this established disorder. In a genuine search for a better world, some turn to Marxism as an alternative. Even some Christians, longing for justice and equality, and trying to free present-day society from its idols and to change human relationships, seek to harmonize Marxism with the Gospel. There are, however, grave dangers in this undertaking. There are some basic elements of Marxist ideology which Christians must reject. We cannot accept the denial of God's existence and intervention in history, the rejection of man's spiritual nature and destiny, the tendency to see in the person only an economic function, the dialectic of violence as the means of social change, and the absorption of individual freedom in a collective social order.[17] As disciples of Christ, we cannot accept the idea that a paradise, an Ideal City, can be fully created here on earth. The Kingdom promised by Christ reaches far beyond this world and calls people to renew themselves unendingly in the spirit of the Risen Lord. You will therefore understand our concern that the Marxist ideology is spreading, especially among youth and activist groups.

16. Nevertheless, some Christians engaged in struggles for justice use what is commonly called "Marxist analysis." This approach can help to identify certain injustices and structures of exploitation. However, there is a tendency in Marxist analysis to reduce every social struggle to two main actors—exploiter-exploited, dominators-oppressed, masters-slaves. We cannot deny that some class struggles have brought about important social changes in history. Grave consequences arise, however, when such struggles are founded on a narrow vision of man, promote hatred and violence and give rise to a new kind of oppression. In proclaiming the gospel message of justice and love, Christians speak of man as an image of God with inalienable rights of which he must not be robbed in any social change. Christ's plan is that, even in the midst of real struggles, all people should undergo conversion of hearts and attitudes, so that they may *"become new"* and remake the social, economic and political structures that cause human suffering.

Christian Pathways

17. Amid the conflicts and contradictions that now separate and oppress people, we as Christians must strive to distinguish the promises of God's Kingdom from human utopias and ideologies, no matter how worthy. Many people see clearly that today's dominant ideologies, whether capitalism or Marxism, contradict gospel values. Throughout the world these ideologies are expressed in many different social models, all of which fail to meet human needs adequately. This is shown by the fact that a search for new social values, goals and structures is a mark of the times. In Canada and elsewhere, much human effort is going into study, debate and action to shape the future. In these events, God calls you to break out of inadequate patterns of thinking and acting, to live new lives, to join all men in building a new society in which there is a real freedom based on love and justice.

18. In your neighbourhood you may be faced with a variety of options and strategies. Some people will choose to continue reforming our present capitalist system in the light of the Gospel. Others will choose to participate in socialist movements, trying to reconcile them with the teachings of Jesus. And still others, rejecting these options, will become involved in searching for some alternative socio-economic order based on gospel principles. As people pursue these different strategies, there is bound to be within the Christian community tension and debate which can be a healthy process for change. But one thing is certain: No option is valid that does not unite people in efforts for the creation of a society based on justice.

Future Action

19. We wish to express in the strongest possible way our continued support for the growing number of Christians engaged in struggles for justice. In the next two years, we intend to initiate a pastoral plan of action for the purpose of encouraging more members of the Catholic community to become actively involved in creating a socio-economic order based on justice. We, therefore, urge people in Christian communities to become involved in the following steps:

- Review the six guidelines and study questions for Christian action outlined in the 1976 Labour Day Message, "From Words to Action."[18] The guidelines contain practical suggestions whereby Christians can become actively involved in struggles for justice going on in local communities. The formation of local study/action groups on problems of injustice is essential.
- Participate in study/action projects which may be launched next year in each diocese and region. Next spring, a working document will be issued which is designed to stimulate greater Christian awareness and action in each region on the vital issues of injustice in Canada and the Third World.
- Participate in regional conferences on social justice. During the next two years, there will be several opportunities for members of the Catholic community to come together on a regional basis for the purpose of sharing analyses and experiences on various problems of injustice and developing strategies for necessary social change in this country.

True Development

20. Ten years ago, describing true human progress in his encyclical *Populorum Progressio*, Paul VI appealed for universal solidarity among mankind. This solidarity must allow all peoples to develop their full personality as individuals and as groups. Such integral development calls for self-reliant peoples who will be the artisans of their own development, whose concern will be to build their solidarity, putting into it the best of themselves.[19] Different models of society can be built from gospel values of love, justice and equality; but no social order built without these values can meet fully the legitimate aspirations of all mankind. Christians inspired by these values, who in the tradition of the prophets dedicate themselves to the cause of authentic social development, are witnesses to hope in the world of today.

Appendix 4

Unemployment: The Human Costs

Canadian Conference of Catholic Bishops January 1980

"I'm just no good. I can't pay the bills and take care of my family."

—a father

"How many times can you be told you are not wanted and still keep your self-respect?"

—a single woman

"No wonder my husband drinks. He sees the children going without good food and clothing while the bills keep piling up. He can't face that day in and day out."

—a mother

"They tell us to get an education, but if the unemployment situation keeps up, we won't be able to get jobs anyway, so why try?"

—a young student

1. These statements illustrate the human suffering experienced by the unemployed in our country today. They add a sense of urgency to the battery of monthly statistics on unemployment. Out of a work force of over

10 million in Canada, close to 800,000 people are jobless. In spite of the creation of new employment, the problem has become more serious in recent years than at any other period since the 1930s.[1] The unemployment situation today illustrates one of the major social issues identified in our recent pastoral program, *Witness to Justice.*[2] It also reflects the need for fundamental social change, which we stated in our message, "A Society to Be Transformed."[3]

2. In the context of our pastoral program, *Witness to Justice*, we intend once again to speak out against the realities of unemployment as a particular example of justice. As pastoral leaders of the Catholic Church in Canada, we invite our brothers and sisters of the Christian community to join us in raising questions about the human realities of unemployment, its underlying causes, the distortion of social values and the possibilities for community action. In recent years, the bishops of Quebec have made several pastoral statements on the problem of unemployment. Today, our concern is to address the phenomenon of unemployment in the whole of Canada. We hope that our reflections will bring some clarity to the public debate about this crucial issue and make some contribution toward overcoming the situation of injustice faced by the unemployed today.[4]

I.
Unemployment: Human Realities

3. In moving beyond the maze of statistics and graphs, it becomes clear that the problem of rising unemployment is hurting certain people and certain regions more than others in Canada. For example, unemployment generally hits the working class (e.g., blue-collar workers) more so than the middle class (e.g., professional people).[5] It is more common today among women than men.[6] And young people, particularly those entering the work force for the first time, are experiencing a much higher jobless rate than adults.[7] At the same time, unemployment is more heavily concentrated in certain regions of the country than in others. The Atlantic provinces, for example, experience a jobless rate which is two and three times that of Ontario and the Prairies.[8] And, in every province, there are regions and communities which always run the risk of high unemployment because of boom-and-bust cycles of economic development.

4. As emphasized in previous pastoral statements, the human and social costs of continuing unemployment are themselves staggering.[9] There is the economic strain on family life that comes with the sudden drop in purchasing power and the possibility of indebtedness. There is the psychological strain that comes from a loss of feelings of self-worth coupled with feelings of anxiety, frustration and bitterness. As a result, unemployment has meant lower productivity in the economy, reduction in public revenues and increasing social welfare costs. And these problems, in turn, are further intensified by cutbacks in social services (including unemployment insurance benefits). Today, as unemployment threatens to become a more or less permanent fact of life in our economy, a substantial portion of our population is in danger of becoming more marginalized and disillusioned.[10]

5. For Christians, human labour has always had a special value and meaning. The activity of work calls upon the creative spirit of the person and his or her capacity to cooperate with other members of the community or society. In doing so, people realize their human dignity. It is through their work that men and women are able to support themselves and their families. By interacting with fellow workers in a common task, people have an opportunity to further develop their personalities and sense of self-worth. In this way, people are able to participate in building up their society and give meaning to their existence as human beings. It was Jesus Christ himself "who conferred an eminent dignity on labour when, at Nazareth, he worked with his own hands."[11] And when men and women offer their labour to God, they become "associated with the redemptive work itself of Jesus Christ."[12] Thus, the human activity of work itself, to earn a living that provides the basic needs required for a decent human life, is already part of God's plan and will for mankind.[13]

6. This human vocation cannot be achieved without the right of each person to work and thereby contribute to the development of society and its well-being. Today, the dignity of increasing numbers of people is being violated by the very fact that they are unable to fully exercise these basic human rights. As a result, diverse forms of alienation have emerged. The many thousands of jobless people, unable to participate in the production and development of our society, find themselves alienated from their fellow citizens. At the same time, many workers find that new technologies and relationships in their industry have made their jobs virtually meaningless.[14] And some workers, engaged in the production of wasteful or destructive products for our consumer society, question the value and meaning of their work.[15] While technological advances and economic growth may provide the material for human progress, they cannot, in themselves, bring it about.[16]

II.
Unemployment: Underlying Causes

7. It is not easy for each and every one of us to come to grips with the causes of continuing unemployment. Who is responsible?[17] Some people tend to put the blame on the unemployed themselves. It is often said, for example, that there are plenty of jobs to go around and that the unemployed are "too lazy" or "too choosy." Undoubtedly, this is true in some individual cases. Yet the fact remains that there has been only one job available for every twenty people looking for work in recent years.[18]

Moreover, most of the new jobs being created are for white-collar workers in service industries rather than for blue-collar workers, who are experiencing higher rates of unemployment.

8. There is also a tendency to put the blame on the large number of women and immigrants entering the labour market. However, women and immigrants have the same right as other people to earn a living and to fulfill their human aspirations. The rising cost of living itself, for example, has compelled many women to seek jobs outside the home.[19] Indeed, many women have had to enter the job market out of economic necessity in order to provide support for their families.[20] There are, of course, some people who, caught up in our consumer way of life, take on extra jobs simply to earn more money for luxury expenses. At the same time, many immigrants and refugees are allowed into Canada each year simply because they will take on low-paying jobs or they have the skills for certain jobs that nobody else has in this country. For the most part, however, the factors identified above are not the principal reasons for continuing unemployment. Thus, we are compelled to search further for the real causes of this social disease.

9. We recognize that the problems of continuing unemployment are complex, that they are related to the global economy and that there are no instant or magic solutions. As bishops, we do not claim to be technical experts in economic matters. However, it is our responsibility to invite fellow Christians to take part in identifying the causes of unemployment and seeking solutions. To this end, it is important to examine critically various economic, political and social explanations for continuing unemployment. Among those often identified by specialists are the following causes:[21]

- the concentration of the country's economic power in the hands of a small number of corporations, which has made it difficult to develop labour-intensive industrial strategies that generate thousands of new jobs;[22]

- the continued centralization of the majority of job-producing industries in our major metropolitan areas, which contributes to growing problems of unemployment and economic disparities in several other regions of the country;[23]
- the high levels of foreign ownership and control of Canada's principal industries, which generally put Canadian workers in a vulnerable position during times of economic recession, subject to plant shutdowns and layoffs;[24]
- the orientation of our economy toward exporting Canada's natural resources (gas, timber, coal and other minerals) rather than manufacturing them into finished products, thereby giving up new employment opportunities;[25]
- the large investments of capital in high-technology industrial projects (e.g., pipelines, hydroelectric projects), which may increase our gross national product but produce relatively few permanent jobs;[26]
- the prolongation of lockouts and strikes which result in a loss of productivity and aggravate conditions of unemployment in some regions of the country.

III.
Unemployment: Social Devaluation

10. Together, these and related causes of unemployment point to the more fundamental crises that exist in the values and priorities of our society. Indeed, unemployment is not simply a political or economic or social problem. It is a profoundly moral and spiritual problem in our times. As Pope John Paul II reminds us, the "plague of unemployment" is symptomatic of a basic "moral disorder."[27] We are called, therefore, to examine the basic values and attitudes that motivate the economic and political activities which make our society what it is today.

11. The primary purpose of any economic system, the Church has consistently taught, should be to serve the basic needs required by all people for a more fully human life.[28] In Canada today, despite the many efforts to deal with the urgent needs of people, our society is still a long way from achieving this principal goal. As we have stated in previous messages, the persistence of poverty, unemployment, regional disparities and a variety of related social problems demonstrates that there is something wrong with our social and economic order.[29] It fails to serve the basic needs of all the people. As a consequence, the poorest and the weakest members of our society are made to suffer most.

12. The human realities of unemployment raise vital questions about the values and priorities of our social order. As a modern capitalist society, have we reached the point where greater priority is placed on the value of machines rather than on the value of human labour? Where maximizing profits and growth takes precedence over the goal of serving real human needs? Where protecting private property exists to the detriment of the right to work for thousands of people? Indeed, are we moving toward the point in our society where, as the Holy Father warns, mankind is in danger of becoming "the slave of things, the slave of his own products, the slave of economic systems, the slave of production"?[30]

13. As Christians, we have an alternative vision of mankind and society. The Gospel calls us to prepare for God's Kingdom by participating in the building of a society that is truly based on justice and love. In Canada today, this vision includes a more equitable redistribution of wealth and power among all the people and the development of this country's resources to serve basic human needs.[31] It entails the creation of authentic human communities in which people live and work together in a lifestyle of "caring, sparing and sharing."[32] And this, in turn, requires that greater priority be placed on the value of human labour in our economic life and the creation of socially useful work so that people can truly contribute to the development of a just society.

IV. Unemployment: Community Action

14. We Christians should not stand idly by while thousands of our brothers and sisters are being deprived of their human dignity through unemployment. While there are no instant or magic solutions, it is important that we join together with other people of good will in a common search for strategies and actions to overcome this disease of unemployment that plagues our society. A major task, in the long run, is the development of alternative industrial strategies designed to serve the human needs of all people in this country.[33] This would require effective measures to increase the self-sufficiency of Canada's industries, strengthen the manufacturing sector and other job-producing industries, redistribute capital for industrial development in underdeveloped regions and enhance community ownership and control of local industries. In so doing, emphasis should be placed on recognizing the dignity of human labour through the creation of socially useful work.

15. The long-range task of developing alternative industrial strategies requires study and action by people of good will in local and regional communities throughout this country. As a step in this direction, we encourage more local Christian communities to become involved in a process of:

- Becoming aware of the local realities and experiences of unemployment. This includes being present with unemployed workers, listening to their problems and identifying current and future job needs in your region.
- Analyzing the basic causes of unemployment in your region. This includes some reflection on the structural causes of unemployment to be found in our present economy, which were noted above.

- Making some ethical judgments about the realities and causes of unemployment. This includes some reflection and education on the Christian meaning of human labour and the primary goal of an economic order as serving human needs (in parishes, families, schools and community groups).
- Supporting the specific struggles of unemployed workers in your region. This includes moral and financial support for activities aimed at creating new jobs, obtaining job security for workers, planning shorter work weeks and generating public awareness about the realities and causes of unemployment.
- Participating in efforts to develop alternative industrial strategies in your region. This includes assessing the economic potential of your region, developing alternative plans for economic development and pressing local governments and corporations to change their priorities and industrial strategies.
- Increasing community ownership and control of industries, where desirable. This includes the promotion of cooperatives, worker-controlled industries and other initiatives to develop more effective community participation and control of economic life in your region.

16. In offering these suggestions, we recognize that in different parts of the country, Christian groups are already engaged in study and action on the complex problems of unemployment and industrial strategies. In several cases, Christians are hard at work on these issues through participation in the activities of their local labour union, coalition for full employment or small producer association.[34] In other situations, Christian communities have initiated study-action projects, notably in Newfoundland, Quebec and Nova Scotia, concerning regional problems of unemployment.[35] In each of these cases, it is important to note that Christians are directly involved with the victims of injustice—the unemployed, the exploited worker, the small producer—and others who have been marginalized in our economy. Together, these and related models for study and action may, in turn, provide further insights on how Christians can become more directly engaged in acting on the problems of unemployment and developing alternative industrial strategies in local communities or regions.[36]

17. Labour unions, in addition to government and business, clearly have a vital role to play in developing strategies for full employment in our society.[37] Today, a major concern of many unions in labour-management negotiations is job security for their own workers. Yet, major problems are evident. On the one hand, the prolonged strikes of some powerful labour unions have aggravated conditions of unemployment in certain regions of the country. On the other hand, the existence of large numbers of unemployed is frequently used by companies as an instrument to impose lower wage settlements and working conditions on their workers. It must also be remembered that close to 60 per cent of Canada's work force is unorganized and thus unable to protect their employment aspirations. We therefore urge labour unions not only to seek job security for their own workers but to join ranks with the unemployed and nonunionized workers in a common strategy to overcome the basic structural causes of unemployment in our society.

Conclusions

18. In the final analysis, the complex problems of unemployment are deeply rooted in the economic order. Bold transformations in the values and priorities of our society will be necessary. As John Paul II reminds us: "This difficult road of the indispensable transformation of the structures of economic life is one on which it will not be easy to go forward without the intervention of a true conversion of mind, will and heart."[38]

19. In this connection, the set of working instruments

recently prepared by our Social Affairs Commission are aimed at helping Christian communities to become more committed to the struggle for social and economic justice.[39] These instruments are designed to provide local Christian animators with some of the tools and resources required to develop study-action projects for the transformation of our society. It is our hope that these initiatives will encourage and assist more Christians to travel along the difficult road of building a new society based on justice and love. Finally, we pray, Lord, that you will instill in your people the courage and the strength to become true witnesses for justice in our times.

Notes

1: Ethical Reflections on the Economic Crisis

[1] Among the more recent pastoral statements, see Episcopal Commission for Social Affairs, "Unemployment: The Human Costs," Canadian Conference of Catholic Bishops (CCCB), 1980 [reprinted in the appendix of this book]; Comité des affaires sociales, "Luttes des travailleurs en temps de crise et les jeunes face à la crise," Assemblée des évêques du Québec, 1982. For an ethical reflection on the economic crisis in France, see the recent statement of the bishops of France, "Pour des nouveaux modes de vie," Déclarations du Conseil permanent de l'Episcopat sur la conjoncture économique et sociale, 1982.

[2] Luke 4:16-19, 7:22; Matthew 11:4-6.

[3] Matthew 25:40.

[4] John Paul II, *Laborem Exercens*, nn. 4, 6, 9, 24, 25, 26.

[5] "Unemployment: The Human Costs," n. 5.

[6] *Laborem Exercens,* n. 26.

[7] "Unemployment: The Human Costs," n. 15.

[8] See, for example, John Paul II, *Laborem Exercens,* 1981; John Paul II, *Redemptor Hominis*, 1979; Paul VI, *Octogesima Adveniens*, 1971; Paul VI, *Populorum Progressio*, 1967; World Synod of Bishops, *Justice in the World*, 1971.

[9] See, for example, A.G. Frank, *Crisis in the World*

Economy (New York: Holmes and Meier, 1980); Samir Amin, et al, *La crise, quelle crise? Dynamique de la crise mondiale* (Paris: Maspéro, 1982); S. Rousseau, *Capitalism and Catastrophe: A Critical Appraisal of the Limits to Capitalism* (Cambridge: *Cambridge University Press, 1979); Social Analysis: Linking Faith and Justice* (Washington, D.C.: Centre of Concern, 1980); *La crise économique et sa gestion*, Actes du collogue de l'Association d'économie politique, tenu à l'Université du Québec à Montréal (Montréal: Boréal Express, 1982); Cy Gonick, *Inflation or Depression: An Analysis of the Continuing Crisis in the Canadian Economy* (Toronto: Lorimer, 1975).

[10] See, for examplc, forecasts of the Conference Board of Canada, November 1982. Their forecasts predict moderate recovery with greater unemployment. (With forecasts of economic recovery for 1983 and 1984, unemployment is forecast at 12.7% for 1983 and 11.4% for 1984.)

[11] Observers point out that the highly capital-intensive nature of modern weapons manufacture creates a more rapid rate of technological obsolescence of fixed-capital and thus leads to greater inflationary pressures and higher unemployment. See M. Kaldor, "The Role of Military Technology in Industrial Development," UN Group of Government Experts on the Relationship of Disarmament and Development, May 1980. For a more extensive analysis of this question, see A. Eide and M. Thee, eds., *Problems of Contemporary Militarism* (London, 1980).

[12] See, for example, *La crise économique et sa gestion*, Part I, "La crisc actuelle des societés capitalistes."

[13] John Paul II, *Laborem Exercens*, no. 12, on the "priority of labour." For a commentary, see G. Baum, *The Priority of Labour* (New York, N.Y.: Paulist Press, 1982).

[14] John Paul II, *Laborem Exercens*, no. 13, particularly comments on the error of "economism" and "materialism."

[15] John Paul II, *Laborem Exercens*, no. 5.

[16] See CCCB, "A Society to Be Transformed," 1977 [reprinted in the appendix of this book]; Paul VI, *Populorum Progressio*, no. 33 and no. 57.

[17] For analysis of global disparities, see Brandt Commission Report, *North-South: A Program for Survival*, 1980. For data on disparities in Canada, see *Income Distribution by Size in Canada, Statistics Canada*, 1980. For more extended analysis, see J. Harp and J.R. Hofley, eds., *Structured Inequality in Canada* (Scarborough: Prentice-Hall, 1980).

[18] See the budget statements of the Hon. Allan MacEachen, November 1981 and 28 June 1982, plus the recent statement on the economy by the Hon. Marc Lalonde, 29 October 1982.

[19] See budget statement of Hon. Allan MacEachen, 28 June 1982. Finance Department officials have stated that the 6 and 5 program will have the "unintended effect of transferring income from wages to profits" (see Toronto *Globe and Mail*, 28 August 1982).

[20] It should be noted, for example, that: (1) people earning $18,000, who can least afford reductions in their incomes below the inflation rate, are subjected to the same rate of control as people earning $50,000 salaries or more, who could afford an income freeze; (2) it is estimated that approximately 30% of the total Net National Income generated in Canada (1980) came in the form of dividends, interest, and other investment income rather than wages and salaries which are subject to controls.

[21] See concerns expressed by the Canadian Labour Congress in their "Statement on Economic Policy," 8 July 1982. For a further perspective see, "Wage Controls Won't Work," *Public Employee*, Fall, 1982. See

also, the report of the Confédération des syndicats nationaux (CSN), "Du travail pour tout le monde," février 1982.

[22] See "Unemployment: The Human Costs," n. 12.

[23] See "Unemployment: The Human Costs," nn. 9, 14.

[24] For examples of proposed industrial strategies, see Canadian Labour Congress, *Economic Policy Statement*, May 1982. See also the recent proposals of the Confédération des syndicats nationaux, *La Presse*, 18 November 1982.

[25] As an example of thinking about alternative directions, see J.P. Wogaman, *The Great Economic Debate* (London: SCM Press, 1977).

[26] See, for example, the following Science Council of Canada reports: *The Weakest Link: A Technological Perspective on Canadian Industrial Underdevelopment; Forging the Links: A Technological Policy for Canada; Hard Times/Hard Choices: Technology and the Balance of Payments.*

[27] For references to "true community," see Rt. Hon. Pierre E. Trudeau, *Statements on the Economy*, parts I, III.

2: The Shift in Catholic Social Teaching

[1] Donald Door, *Option for the Poor: A Hundred Years of Vatican Social Teaching* (Maryknoll, N.Y.: Orbis Books, 1983). See also G. Baum, "Faith and Liberation: Development Since Vatican II," in *Vatican II: Open Questions and New Horizons*, ed. Gerald Fagin (Wilmington, Delaware: Michael Glazier, 1984), and "Shift to the Left: Recent Catholic Social Teaching," in the forthcoming *Religion and Economics*, ed. Irving Hexham (Vancouver, B.C.: Fraser Institute).

[2] A. R. Vidler, *A Century of Social Catholicism: 1820-1920* (London: SPCK, 1964); also G. Baum, *Catholics and Canadian Socialism*, (Toronto: Lorimer, 1980).

[3] Charles Taylor, *Radical Tories: The Conservative Tradition in Canada*, (Toronto: Anansi, 1982). See also Gad Horowitz, "Conservatism, Liberalism, and Socialism," *The Canadian Journal of Economics and Political Science*, vol. 32, no. 2 (1966).

[4] For the Medellin documents, see J. Gremillion, ed., *The Gospel of Peace and Justice* (Maryknoll, N.Y.: Orbis Books, 1976), pp. 445-76. The liberationist perspective is found especially in the section, "Peace," pp. 455-63.

[5] For *Octogesima Adveniens*, see J. Grimillion, *op. cit.*, pp. 485-512. Papal documents are divided into numbered paragraphs. The reference to socialism is found in n. 31.

[6] *Octogesima Adveniens*, ibid., nn. 32-33.

[7] For *Justitia in Mundo*, see J. Gremillion, *op. cit.*, pp. 513-29. The liberationist perspective is found in nn. 3-6.

[8] Cardinal Flahiff's address is published in a booklet, *Witness to Justice: Some Statements by the Canadian Catholic Bishops*, (Canadian Catholic Organization for Justice and Peace, no date), pp. 1-3.

[9] *Laborem Exercens* is found in the appendix of G. Baum, *The Priority of Labour* (New York, N.Y.: Paulist Press, 1982). For the reference to solidarity, see n. 8.

[10] Richard Allen, *The Social Passion: Religion and Social Reform in Canada 1914-28* (Toronto: University of Toronto Press, 1973).

[11] For a detailed treatment, see G. Baum, "Beginnings of a Canadian Catholic Social Theory," in the forthcoming *Political Thought in French and English Canada*, ed. Stephen Brooks (Toronto: Clarke Irwin).

[12] See Tony Clarke, "Communities for Justice," *The Ecumenist*, vol. 19 (1981), pp. 17-25.

[13] See Bill Smith, *The Church and Politics in Chile* (Princeton, N.J.: Princeton University Press, 1982), pp. 86-164.

[14] Mel Peil, *Breaking Bread: The Catholic Worker and the Origin of Catholic Radicalism* (Philadelphia, Pa.: Temple University Press, 1982).

[15] When the Canadian cooperatives in the Thirties and Forties became large and successful, they became conservative and followed policies of "business as usual." See Ian MacPherson, *Each for All: A History of the Cooperative Movement in English Canada, 1900-1945* (Toronto: Macmillan, 1979), pp. 213-15.

[16] For the earlier papal view of capitalism, see Donal Dorr, *Option for the Poor* (Maryknoll, N.Y.: Orbis Books, 1983), pp. 14-20, 62-64, 79-81.

[17] For the final document of the Puebla Conference, see *Puebla and Beyond*, eds. J. Eagleson and P. Scharper (Maryknoll, N.Y.: Orbis books, 1979). The definition of "the option for the poor" is found on p. 264, nn. 1134-40.

[18] *Quadragesimo Anno*, n. 65. See also the article "Co-determination," in *The New Catholic Encyclopedia.*

[19] G. Baum, *The Priority of Labour* (New York, N.Y.: Paulist Press, 1982), pp. 22-40.

[20] Ibid., pp. 45-46.

[21] For a similar analysis of capitalism, see J. Holland and P. Henriot, *Social Analysis: Linking Faith and Justice* (Maryknoll, N.Y.: Orbis Books, 1983), pp. 46-60.

[22] The report of the Canadian churches is published in *The Ecumenist*, vol. 21 (1983), pp. 89-94. The quotation is found on p. 91.

[23] S. Torres and J. Eagleson, eds., *The Challenge of Basic Christian Communities* (Maryknoll, N.Y.: Orbis Books, 1981).

[24] G. Anderson, ed., *Witnessing to the Kingdom* (Maryknoll, N.Y.: Orbis Books, 1982); C. Geffré and G. Gutierrez, eds., *The Mystical and Political Dimension of the Christian Faith* (New York, N.Y.: Herder & Herder, 1974); P. Erdozain, *Archbishop Romero: Martyr of Salvador* (Maryknoll, Orbis Books, 1980); T.

Cabestrero, *Mystic of Liberation* (New York, N.Y.: Orbis Books, 1981).

[25] See G. Baum, "The First Encyclical," *The Ecumenist*, vol. 17, 1979, pp. 55-59.

[26] *Globe and Mail*, 22 January 1983.

[27] G. Baum, *Catholics and Canadian Socialism* (Toronto: Lorimer, 1980), pp. 47-53.

[28] G. Baum, *Religion and Alienation* (New York, N.Y.: Paulist Press, 1975), pp. 99-107.

[29] *Quadragesimo Anno*, n. 114.

[30] Baum, *The Priority of Labour*, pp. 9-30.

[31] See especially the Labour Day Message 1974, "Sharing Daily Bread." See also the reference in "A Society to Be Transformed," n. 19, printed in the appendix.

[32] Social Affairs Commission, *Witness to Justice* (Ottawa: CCCB, 1979), pp. 85-119.

3: Do Canada's Bishops Make Economic Sense?*

[1] The text of the governor's speech is reprinted in the *Bank of Canada Review*, December 1982. This publication provides statistical information about the Canadian economy. Unless otherwise indicated, the review (various issues) is the source for the figures given in this commentary.

[2] As reported by Canadian Press; see the *Ottawa Citizen*, 12 January 1983.

[3] The statement of the fourteen groups was published in *Le Devoir*, 13 January 1983.

[4] In a widely reported statement (Empire Club, Toronto, 13 January 1983), Thomas d'Acquino,

---

* The assistance and encouragement provided by Gregory Baum, Norman Cameron, Irene Spry, Joy Woolfrey, David Ross, Fred Caloren, Michael McBane and Bob Clarke in the preparation of this commentary, are gratefully acknowledged. In addition, the editorial counsel of Ted Mumford was greatly appreciated.

president, Business Council on National Issues, made this point. The council, composed of chief executives, is broadly representative of the business community. His views were challenged by an editorial in the *Globe and Mail* (15 January 1983) and by Southam columnist Don McGillivary (*Ottawa Citizen*, 17 January 1983).

[5] International Monetary Fund (IMF), *World Economic Outlook* (Washington, 1982), p. 150.

[6] This view was articulated by the chief executive officer of the Royal Bank of Canada in his appearance before the House of Commons Committee (Finance, Trade and Economic Affairs) investigating the profit situation of the chartered banks. See the *Minutes of Proceedings*... (10 June 1982), issue no. 103.

[7] In *La Presse* (23 June 1982, p. B1) Jean Poulain argues that from May 1981 to May 1982 inflation in those sectors where government pricing decisions were important averaged 14.4%. The increase in the CPI was 11.8% for the same period. Moreover, he claims that about 57% of the CPI is affected principally by governments. The Quebec Employers Council (CPQ) have pointed out that indirect taxes increased by 27.2% in 1982. See *La Presse* (5 January 1983).

[8] This argument is examined (and found wanting) in a publication of the Canadian Centre for Policy Alternatives (CCPA), *Trade Unions and Inflation,* by Peter Warrian and David Wolfe (Ottawa, 1982).

[9] Peter Newman, in an appendix to *The Canadian Establishment,* vol. 2 (Toronto: McClelland and Stewart, 1981), has documented some of the most important takeovers (pp. 434-489). Between 1975 and 1981, over 250 major transactions occurred.

[10] Writing in the *Financial Post* (22 January 1983, p. 8), economist John McCallum, commenting on an OECD report, argued that "much of our current recession is made in Canada."

[11] Martin Mittelstaedt in the *Globe and Mail* (12

November 1982) found this "worrisome assessment" from various observers in the financial community. Peter Cook, *Globe and Mail* (13 November 1982), wrote that "the major players in the capital markets have every reason to be nervous."

[12] Diane Bellemare and Lise Poulin-Simon, *Le Plein emploi: Pourquoi?* (Montreal: Les Presses de l'Université du Québec, 1983).

[13] See the analysis by Thomas Walkom, *Globe and Mail*, 9 July 1983. The Social Planning Council of Metropolitan Toronto has studied these questions. Its estimate for discouraged workers was that in May 1983 they numbered 470,000!

[14] This was the position taken by the finance minister at the time of the November 1981 budget. See *The Current Economic Situation and Prospects for the Canadian Economy in the Short and Medium Term* (Ottawa: Department of Finance, 1981).

[15] This is the position of the so-called neo-conservatives. See the article by Walter Block, senior economist, the Fraser Institute, *Financial Post*, 9 April 1983, p. 8.

[16] Bob Kuttner, "The Declining Middle," *Atlantic Monthly*, July 1983; Ed Finn, "Decline of the Middle Class," *The Facts*, Publication of the Canadian Union of Public Employees (CUPE), November 1983.

[17] As reported by Ronald Anderson, *Globe and Mail,* 15 July 1983.

[18] Ian Miles, "Joblessness and Health," *World Press Review*, July 1983.

[19] This is paraphrased from Juan-Luis Gallegos, *Le Devoir*, 5 July 1983.

[20] F. Frobel, J. Heinrichs and O. Krege, *The New International Division of Labour* (Cambridge, England: Cambridge University Press, 1980).

[21] The evidence linking increases in wages to fluctuations in private investment is weak. See Duncan Cameron, "Wage Earners, the Liberals and the Canadian Economy," *Our Generation*, Spring 1983.

[22] Ed Finn, "Wage Control Cancer Spreads," *The Facts*, November 1982, and "Bill C-124 Anti-Union Legislation," *The Facts*, August-September 1982.

[23] See for instance the editorials "Economic Sermon," *Globe and Mail*, 5 January 1983, and "The Bishops' Muddled Message," *Financial Times*, 10 January 1983.

[24] This was the view of Quebec's employer group (CPQ). See the Montreal *Gazette*, 5 January 1983.

[25] This was the main message of the statement by Thomas d'Acquino (see note 4). He states: "Profits are, for the most part, put to work to keep the engines of industry running and thereby to employ and to pay people, and to pay taxes."

[26] See, for instance, the views of a professor of business and public policy at Harvard's Kennedy School of Government: Robert B. Reich, *The Next American Frontier* (New York: Times Books, 1983).

[27] See the analysis by John Cruickshank, *Globe and Mail*, 22 July 1983.

[28] Canada, Department of Finance, *Economic Development for Canada in the 1980's* (Ottawa, November 1981).

[29] See Duncan Cameron, "L'État canadien, la restructuration économique, et la politique extérieure," in *Cahiers de l'ACFAS* No. 16 (Montreal, 1983).

[30] On world trade and finance, see Duncan Cameron, "Order and Disorder in the World Economy," *Studies in Political Economy*, no. 11 (Summer 1983).

[31] See the series of articles by Cy Gonick, *Winnipeg Free Press*, February 1983.

[32] See the report by Ann Silversides, *Globe and Mail*, 10 September 1983.

[33] Remi de Roo, "What's Wrong with Canada?" *Policy Alternatives*, Spring-Summer, 1982.

[34] See Marsha Hewitt, "The Canadian Bishops' Statement," *Our Generation*, Spring 1983.

Appendix 1: Northern Development: At What Cost?

[1] These reflections and judgments are based on a variety of consultations with people concerned with the future development of the Canadian North. See in particular a recent work by Louis-Edmond Hamelin, "Nordicité canadienne" (Montreal: H.M.H., 1975).

[2] For example, see Eric Gourdeau, "The People of the Canadian North," and "Impressions of the Land," in *Arctic Alternatives* (Ottawa: Canadian Arctic Resources Committee, 1973).

[3] The particular phrase is the title of a documentary produced by the National Film Board and a direct quote from the Cree Indian people of the Mistassini area in Northern Quebec. Variations of this theme are frequently expressed by Native Peoples, throughout the North.

[4] See Lloyd Barber, "The Basis for Native Claims in Canada," Address to the Rotary Club, Yellowknife, NWT, October 1974. Mr. Barber is the Indian claims commissioner for Canada. See also, René Fumoleau, o.m.i., "As Long As This Land Shall Last" (Toronto: McClelland and Stewart, 1975).

[5] See Wade Rowland, *Fueling Canada's Future* (Toronto: Macmillan, 1974), chap. 2.

[6] This concern was expressed in a 11 July 1973 letter to Premier Bourassa by Cardinal Maurice Roy of Quebec, writing as president of the Assemblée des évêques du Québec.

[7] Cf. two comparative articles: *Whose Development?—The Impact of Development on the Native Peoples of Canada and Brazil*; and *What Price Development? Foreign Investment and Resources Extraction in British Columbia and Jamaica*. Both articles are available from the Interchurch Committee for World Development Education, 600 Jarvis St., Toronto.

[8] For example, see *l'Aménagement de la Baie James: Progrès ou désastre?* par le comité pour la défense de

la Baie James, Montréal; *The Churchill Diversion—Time Runs out for the Native People of the North*, available from the Canadian Association in Support of Native Peoples, Ottawa; *Northwest Development: What and For Whom?* available from the Northwest B.C. Conference Committee, Terrace, B.C.

[9] This has been the case with most of the major energy projects in the North to date. A land settlement is currently being negotiated with the Native People of the James Bay region, but these negotiations are taking place *after* the basic industrial plans have been established.

[10] For example, the natives of Nelson House Reserve and South Indian Lake in Northern Manitoba face serious problems of flooding. See "Northern Manitoba: The Project and the People," *Bulletin*, Canadian Association in Support of Native Peoples, December 1974.

[11] For example, during the construction of the Pointed Mountain Pipeline in the Territories, only 30 native people were employed for a maximum of three months, while 320 workers were brought in from the South. In 1970, after the federal government has invested $9 million in Panarctic, it has employed only 6 natives at $1.75 an hour. See Melville Watkins, "Resources and Underdevelopment," in *(Canada) Ltd.*, ed. by Robert M. Laxer (Toronto: McClelland and Stewart, 1973).

[12] *Gaudium et Spes,* n. 69; *Populorum Progressio*, n. 22.

[13] James Wash-shee, president, Indian Brotherhood of the Northwest Territories, cited in the Brotherhood's initial submission to the Berger Inquiry, 1975.

[14] See George Manuel, *The Fourth World* (Toronto: Collier & MacMillan, 1974).

[15] Third Synod of Bishops, 1971, *Justice in the World*, n. 14.

[16] See *An Energy Policy for Canada: Phase I* (Ottawa: Department of Energy, Mines and Resources, 1973).

[17] Ibid., vol. 1, p. 11.

[18] See, for example, Wade Rowland, *Fueling Canada's*

Future; Canadian Arctic Resources Committee, *Gas from the Mackenzie Delta: Now or Later*; James Laxer, *Canada's Energy Crisis;* Pollution Probe at the University of Toronto, *Background Statement on the Arctic,* 28 March 1972, revised 12 April 1972.

[19] Rowland, *Fueling Canada's Future*, p. 44.

[20] Based on statistics provided by Meadows et al, *The Limits to Growth*, a report for the Club of Rome's Project on the Predicament of Mankind, 1972.

[21] Barbara Ward and René Dubois, *Only One Earth* (England: Penguin Books, 1972), p. 44.

[22] See Ivan Illich, *Energy and Equity* (New York: Harper & Row, 1974).

[23] See Mihajlo Mesarovic and Eduard Pestel, *Mankind at the Turning Point*, The Second Report to the Club of Rome.

[24] "Simplicity and Sharing," 1972 Labour Day Message, Canadian Catholic Conference of Bishops. See also Thomas S. Derr, *Ecologie et libération humaine* (Genève: Editions Labor et Fides, 1974).

[25] *Development Demands Justice*, a joint statement by Canadian Church leaders, March 1973.

[26] Canadian Oblate Conference, *The Religious Situation of the Canadian Native People*, November, 1971.

[27] Third Synod of Bishops, 1971, *Justice in the World*, Introduction.

[28] For detailed information, see *Resource Kit on Northern Development*, available at cost, from the Social Affairs Desk, Canadian Catholic Conference, 90 Parent Avenue, Ottawa K1N 7B1.

Appendix 2: From Words to Action

[1] At the Eucharistic Congress in Philadelphia this year [1976], Archbishop Helder Camara called this the "scandal of the century": where rich countries and rich persons go on becoming richer while poor nations and the poor in every nation become ever poorer.

[2] For current examples of loneliness, alienation, etc.,

see *Project Feedback* II "Assessing Everyday Life," V "How People Feel about the 1980s," Canadian Catholic Conference of Bishops.

[3] See Messages des Évêques canadiens à l'occasion de la fête du travail (1956-74), une présentation de Richard Arès, S.J. For copies in English, see the September issue of *Social Thought*, available from the Canadian Catholic Conference, Social Affairs Desk.

[4] For some examples, see *Project Feedback* I "Peoples Social Hopes," Canadian Catholic Conference of Bishops.

[5] *Justice in the World*, Synod III, p. 12 plus *Evangelii Nuntiandi*, article 29.

[6] *Evangelii Nuntiandi,* articles 33, 34, 38, 70.

[7] See *Populorum Progressio*, encyclical of Pope Paul VI, especially article 22.

[8] Especially, "Sharing Daily Bread," 1974 Labour Day Message, and "Northern Development: At What Cost?" 1975 Labour Day Message. Canadian Catholic Conference of Bishops. These statements focused on twin ethical themes of "social justice" and "responsible stewardship" of resources.

[9] Through, for example, participation in active events around the World Population Conference in Bucharest, the World Food Conference in Rome, the Seventh Special Session of the United Nations in New York, the United Nations Conference on Habitat in Vancouver, the United Nations Conference on Trade and Development in Nairobi, plus the annual shareholders meetings of various transnational corporations and meetings with government leaders.

[10] *Justice Demands Action*, a brief presented by the Canadian Church leaders to the prime minister and federal cabinet, 2 March 1976, article 7.

[11] *A New Commandment?* A Pastoral Exhortation for the 1976 Lenten Season, Canadian Catholic Conference of Bishops.

[12] *Octogesima Adveniens*, Letter of Pope Paul to

Cardinal Roy, May 1971, articles 24, 46. See also, *The Church and Human Rights*, Pontifical Commission for Justice and Peace, 1975, especially pp. 49-54.

Appendix 3: A Society to Be Transformed

[1] *Poverty in Canada*, Report of the Special Senate Committee (Ottawa, 1971), p. 11.

[2] *Octogesima Adveniens*, Apostolic Letter of Pope Paul VI to Cardinal Maurice Roy, president of the Council of the Laity and of the Pontifical Commission Justice and Peace, on the occasion of the eightieth anniversary of the Encyclical *Rerum Novarum,* 14 May 1971, n. 48.

[3] Ibid., n. 12.

[4] *Populorum Progressio*, Encyclical Letter of Pope Paul VI on the development of peoples, 26 March 1967, n. 28.

[5] *Gaudium et Spes*, Vatican II Pastoral Constitution on the Church in the Modern World, 7 December 1965, n. 39.

[6] *Evangelii Nuntiandi*, Apostolic Exhortation by Pope Paul VI on evangelization, 8 December 1975, n. 13.

[7] Ibid., n. 2.

[8] See Amos; Jeremiah; Isaiah; Hosea; Psalms 9, 10, 40, 72, 76, 146; Mt. 25:31-46; Mark 10:42-45; Luke 4:18-20; James 1:9; 2:1-13; 5:1-6.

[9] Jn. 13:34; 1 Jn. 4: 7, 11, 16.

[10] 1 Jn. 4:20.

[11] Equality is difficult to attain, but Christians must struggle towards such an ideal. They cannot accept present inequalities as the inevitable outcome of natural selection, as social Darwinists would argue. Instead, they should be guided by insights such as those found in the Acts of the Apostles 2:42-47; 4:32-35, as well as in St. Paul: "That as a matter of equality your abundance at the present time should supply their want, so that their abundance may supply your want, that there may be

equality. As it is written, 'He who gathered much had nothing over, and he who gathered little had no lack' " (2 Cor. 8 13-15). Pope Leo XII, in turn, taught: "...when what necessity demands has been supplied, and one's standing fairly taken thought for, it becomes a duty to give to the indigent out of what remains over" (*Rerum Novarum*, n. 22). And Pius XI added: "A person's superfluous income, that is, income which he does not need to sustain life fittingly and with dignity, is not left wholly to his own free determination (Quadragesimo *Anno*, n. 50).

[12] Gal. 1:5, 6:2.

[13] Matthew 5:1-16.

[14] *Populorum Progressio*, n. 81.

[15] *Octogesima Adveniens*, n. 4.

[16] *Populorum Progressio*, n. 26.

[17] *Octogesima Adveniens*, n. 26.

[18] "From Words to Action," Canadian Conference of Catholic Bishops, 1976 Labour Day Message.

[19] *Populorum Progressio*, n. 43 and following paragraphs.

Appendix 4: Unemployment: The Human Costs

[1] It is difficult to obtain an accurate picture of the number of people who are unemployed. Official statistics do not include the so-called hidden unemployed, the countless numbers of people who have given up looking for work after numerous frustrations.

[2] See the set of working instruments prepared by our Episcopal Commission for Social Affairs, entitled *Witness to Justice: A Society to Be Transformed* (May 1979).

[3] "A Society to Be Transformed," Social Message of the Catholic bishops, 1977.

[4] In the past, Canadian bishops have addressed the problems of unemployment, as, for example, in the 1964 Labour Day Message, "Automation." More recently, the Quebec bishops have issued three pastoral messages: "La dignité de l'homme n'a pas de prix"

(1977); "Discovering the Unemployed as Brethren" (1978); "Les jeunes n'ont past choisi d'être chômeurs" (1979). And a pastoral letter by Bishop A. Carter and Msgr. A. Proulx, "Layoffs by Inco and Falconbridge" (1977), addresses the problem of layoffs in the mining industry at Sudbury, Ontario.

[5] In mid-1977, for example, the *Financial Times* of Canada reported that there were 112,000 fewer manufacturing jobs than one year earlier, which had a direct impact on blue-collar workers.

[6] In September of 1979, for example, the official statistics state that 8.5 per cent of women in the labour force were unemployed, while the figure for men was just 6.2 per cent.

[7] In September of 1979, for example, the jobless rates for those under twenty-five stood at 12.3 per cent, while it was 7.1 per cent for the labour force as a whole, or 5.1 per cent for those over twenty-five.

[8] In September of 1979, the national average stood at 7.4 per cent. The regional breakdown was as follows: Newfoundland, 14.1 per cent; P.E.I., 10.6; New Brunswick, 10.7; Nova Scotia, 10.2; Quebec, 9.1; Ontario, 6.1; Manitoba, 5.0; Saskatchewan, 3.9; Alberta, 3.7; and British Columbia, 7.7. For some insights on the social and economic effects of uneven patterns of development, see, for example, *Une région où règne l'insécurité, le Nord-ouest québecois*, Dossier "vie ouvrière" (Montreal, 1978), n. 127.

[9] In "Discovering the Unemployed as Brethren," the Quebec bishops describe the economic, psychological, moral and social ordeals which unemployed people suffer today.

[10] For a popular discussion of these concerns, see, for example, *Quand ferment les usines*. Dossier "vie ouvrière" (Montreal, 1977), n. 117. A more recent publication on this subject is *Quand ferment les usines*, prepared by le Centre Saint-Pierre Apôtre (Montreal, 1979).

[11] *Gaudium et Spes*, Document of Vatican II on the

Church in the Modern World (7 December 1965), n. 67.

[12] Ibid.

[13] Ibid., nn. 35, 36.

[14] See, for example, R. Blauner, *Alienation and Freedom: The Factory Worker and His Industry* (Chicago: University of Chicago Press, 1964); *Work in America* (Cambridge, Mass.: M.I.T. Press); S. Turkel, ed., *Working People* (Avon, 1975).

[15] For a discussion of wasteful or destructive forms of production in our consumer society, see B. Commoner, *The Closing Circle* (Bantam, 1972).

[16] *Gaudium et Spes*, n. 35.

[17] For a discussion of popular misconceptions about unemployment, see *Unemployment*, Issue 18, United Church of Canada publication.

[18] Cited in *Jobs and People*, the Economic Council of Canada, 1976. This study also concluded that four out of five persons who draw UIC benefits are unemployed for reasons beyond their control, because of layoffs or job termination.

[19] It is now estimated that 57 per cent of Canadian families are dependent on two salaries in order to meet rising costs. The number of working women, or those looking for work, has tripled over the last thirty years. Yet, the jobs that the vast majority of women are generally compelled to take in the labour market tend to offer relatively low wages, unstable employment, few benefits and little opportunity for career development or advancement. In a recent study, *Women and Work: The Second Time Around: A Study of Women Returning to the Work Force* (Ottawa: Canadian Advisory Council on the Status of Women, 1979), M. Pearson concludes that economic necessity is the primary motivating force behind women re-entering the job market. "Inflation has made two incomes essential for many families in order to maintain

economic stability and to provide for future financial security" (p. 9). In the case of poor families living under the poverty line, the study shows that "many low-income families may be beyond the poverty line only because both husband and wife are paid workers. Clearly, these women are breadwinners and the financial stability of their families depends in part on their salaries" (pp. 9-10).

[20] The study *Women and Work: The Second Time Around* points out that "almost 40 percent of all working women are single, divorced, separated or widowed, and therefore must work to support themselves and their families with the necessities of life; all too often, 'frills' are out of the question" (pp. 10-11).

[21] In *Witness to Justice: A Society to Be Transformed*, the CCCB Social Affairs Commission has provided a set of working instruments which may be useful in analyzing many of the economic and political strategies outlined below. See, for example, discussions on : "Global Economy," p. 35; "Concentration of Corporate Power," p. 38; "Centralized Economy," p. 39; "Hinterland Regions," p. 62; "Foreign Ownership," p. 37; "Economic Dependency," p. 37; "Increasing Lay-Offs," p. 50; "Exploitation of Workers," p. 51; "Control of Workers," p. 52; "Southern Impact," p. 70.

[22] For a detailed study on the concentration of economic power in Canada, see Wallace Clement, *The Canadian Corporate Elite: An Analysis of Economic Power* (Toronto: McClelland and Stewart, 1975). For a brief treatment of the subject, see *Who's in Control?* Issue 14, United Church of Canada publication. See also *Gaudium et Spes*, n. 65. For an analysis of economic concentration in Quebec, see Arnaud Sales, *La Bourgeoisie industrielle au Québec* (l'Université de Montréal, 1979).

[23] For an overview of the regional disparities that result from a centralized economy, see Paul Phillips, *Regional Disparities* (Toronto: Lorimer, 1978). See also *Atlantic*

Regional Disparities, prepared by the Social Affairs Commission, Diocese of Charlottetown; *Now That We've Burned Our Boats* (Newfoundland: Peoples' Commission on Unemployment, 1979); A. Dubuc, "Recul de Montréal ou socio-développement du Québec?" in *L'Economie québécoise*, Rodrigue Tremblay (dir.), (Montreal: Presses de l'Université du Québec, Montréal, 1976), pp. 439-49.

[24] A recent study by the Science Council of Canada shows that foreign investment has had a negative effect on Canada's present and future industrial performance. See J.H.N. Britton and J.M. Gilmour, *The Weakest Link* (Ottawa: Supply and Services Canada, 1978). There are many reports and studies illustrating the vulnerability of Canada's economy due to high levels of foreign ownership. The classic work is Kari Levitt's *Silent Surrender: The Multinational Corporation in Canada* (Toronto: Macmillan, 1979).

[25] See, for example, the report of the Science Council, *The Structure of Canadian Industry* (1972), which pointed out that Canada's policies of exporting natural resources has resulted in a new loss of jobs. In this same study, the Science Council also contends that the strengthening of Canada's manufacturing sector is essential to overcoming problems of continuing unemployment. Moreover, the Organization for Economic Cooperation and Development (OECD) reports that Canada now employs a smaller percentage of its labour force in manufacturing than all other industrialized countries except Turkey and Greece.

[26] For a case study of the impact of capital-intensive resource development on workers in Canada, see *Paying the Piper*, prepared by the GATT-Fly Project.

[27] John Paul II, *Redemptor Hominis* (1979), n. 55.

[28] *Gaudium et Spes*, nn. 63, 25; *Populorum Progressio*, encyclical of Pope Paul VI (1978), n. 22.

[29] Canadian bishops, "From Words to Action," Labour

Day Message, 1976, n. 3; and "A Society to Be Transformed," Social Message, 1977.

30 John Paul II, *Redemptor Hominis*, n. 52.

31 "From Words to Action," nn. 3, 7.

32 Canadian bishops, "Simplicity and Sharing," Labour Day Message, 1972.

33 For some insights on alternative economic strategies, see E.F. Schumacher, *Small Is Beautiful* (New York: Harper and Row, 1976), and Henderson, *Creating Alternative Futures*. For an overview of industrial democracy and worker-controlled industries, see David Jenkins, *Job Power: Blue and White Collar Democracy* (New York: Penguin, 1974).

34 The ecumenical project, Ten Days for World Development, has recently launched a three-year education program on the rights and needs of working people, including the problems of unemployment, in Canada and the Third World. See, for example, *Making a Living* (Ten Days for World Development, 600 Jarvis Street, Toronto). In Quebec, le Mouvement des Travailleurs chrétiens and la Jeunesse Ouvrière Catholique are two examples of direct involvement of Christians in the struggles of workers. For further information, contact Mouvement des Travailleurs chrétiens, 7559 boul. St. Laurent, Montréal, and la Jeunesse Ouvrière, 685 Decarie N., Montréal, P.Q.

35 See, for example, *Now That We've Burned Our Boats* (Newfoundland: People's Commission on Unemployment). This is the report of the People's Commission which was organized by labour unions and other regional groups to conduct a public inquiry into the human realities and causes of unemployment in Newfoundland. See also *Working Together: A Report by the National Council of Welfare on Creating New Job Opportunities*, 1978.

36 For an example of alternative industrial strategies in community development, see C. Banville, *Les Opéra-*

tions dignité (Québec: Le Fonds de recherches forestières de l'Université de Laval, 1977).

[37] For previous statements by the Canadian bishops on the important role of labour unions, see "Church's Solidarity with Workers and Victims of Social Injustice," Labour Day Message, 1968; "Social Teachings of the Church," Labour Day Message, 1961.

[38] John Paul II, *Redemptor Hominis*, n. 56.

[39] Episcopal Commission for Social Affairs, *Witness to Justice: A Society to Be Transformed.*

Further Reading

Gregory Baum

Allen, Richard. *The Social Passion: Religion and Social Reform in Canada 1914-28.* Toronto: University of Toronto Press, 1973. A distinguished historian tells the story of the Canadian social gospel up to the Thirties.

Baum, Gregory. *Catholics and Canadian Socialism: Political Thought in the Thirties and Forties.* Toronto: James Lorimer, 1980. This book examines the reaction of Catholics to the social philosophy of the CCF.

Baum, Gregory. *The Priority of Labour.* New York, N.Y.: Paulist Press, 1982. This commentary on Pope John Paul II's encyclical, *Laborem Exercens*, explains the new orientation of Catholic social teaching.

Calvez, Jean-Yves. *The Social Thought of John XXIII.* London, England: Burns and Oates, 1964. In the early Sixties, Pope John opened the windows of the Catholic Church. This book analyzes his new approach to social questions.

Camp, Richard. *The Papal Ideology of Social Reform.* Leiden, Netherlands: E.J. Brill, 1969. A political scientist looks at papal social teaching in the context of European political developments.

Clark, S.D., et al. *Prophecy and Protest: Social Movements in Twentieth-Century Canada.* Toronto: Gage Educational Publishing, 1975. This collection of articles provides useful information on the impact of religion on social change in Canadian society.

Crysdale, Stewart. *The Industrial Struggle and Protestant Ethics in Canada*. Toronto: Ryerson Press, 1961. An analysis of the critical social positions adopted by the Protestant churches in Canada in the first half of the present century.

Dorr, Donal. *Option for the Poor: A Hundred Years of Vatican Social Teaching*. Maryknoll, N.Y.: Orbis Books, 1983. This is the best presentation of the emerging Catholic social teaching. It honestly records the discontinuities and the continuities in this ecclesiastical development.

Gremillion, Joseph, *The Gospel of Peace and Justice: Catholic Social Teaching Since Pope John*. Maryknoll, N.Y.: Orbis Books, 1976. This is the most useful collection of recent ecclesiastical documents on social justice, including Roman and Latin American statements.

Gutierrez, Gustavo. *A Theology of Liberation: History, Politics and Salvation*. Maryknoll, N.Y.: Orbis Books, 1973. Among the growing Latin American literature on liberation theology, this is the most famous volume.

McGovern, Arthur. *Marxism: An American Christian Perspective*. Maryknoll, N.Y.: Orbis Books, 1980. A Catholic social philosopher offers a sympathetic, critical analysis of Marxism and its possible use in Catholic theological thinking.

Smillie, Ben. *Political Theology in the Canadian Context*. Waterloo, Ont.: Wilfred Laurier University Press, 1982. This book contains the proceedings of a theological conference that dealt with the critical impact of Christian values on contemporary Canadian society.

Duncan Cameron

Britton J., and Gilmour, J. *The Weakest Link: A Technological Perspective on Canadian Industrial Under-*

development. Ottawa: Science Council of Canada (Background Study 43), 1978. This study provides a telling account of the negative effects of foreign ownership on technological innovation in Canada.

Caloren, Fred, et al. *Is the Canadian Economy Closing Down?* Montreal: Black Rose Books, 1978. This book presents studies of layoffs and factory closures, unemployment and capitalist crisis, and economic policy. It is well documented and accessible to the general reader.

Crane, David, ed. *Beyond the Monetarists*. Toronto: James Lorimer, 1981. A collection of essays by dissenters (in various degrees) from orthodox views. Other titles in the Canadian Institute for Economy Policy Series may be of interest.

Cunningham, Frank. *Understanding Marxism*. Toronto: Progress Books, 1977. Many people, but especially critics of the bishops who believe them to be tainted by "Marxism," would be well advised to further their understanding of this important subject. This account is sympathetic.

Deane, Phyllis. *The Evolution of Economic Ideas*. Cambridge, England: Cambridge University Press, 1978. A short history which requires concentrated study.

Harrington, Michael. *The Twilight of Capitalism*. New York, N.Y.: Touchstone Books, 1976. An American democratic socialist makes a case against capitalism.

Heilbroner, Robert. *The Making of Economic Society*. Englewood Cliffs, New Jersey: Prentice-Hall, 1962. For the beginning reader this is one of the most accessible and sensible books available.

Kindleberger, Charles P. *Manias, Panics and Crashes*. London, England: Papermac, 1981. A study which puts the financial instability of capitalism in historical perspective.

Lemeche, S.Q., ed. "The Challenge of Inflation and Unemployment." Laidler, D. ed. "Has Monetarism Failed?" *Canadian Public Policy*, no. 7 (April 1981).

This special issue provides two series of articles by specialists with introductions by the editors.

Levitt, Kari. *Silent Surrender: The Multinational Corporation in Canada*. Toronto: Macmillan, 1970. This book remains the clearest statement available of the problems associated with foreign investment in Canada.

Macpherson, C.B. *The Life and Times of Liberal Democracy*. Toronto: Oxford University Press, 1977. Democracy is invoked by both the bishops and their critics. This treatment is quite simply one of the best small books on politics published in the last forty years. Will repay the effort.

Moggridge, D.E. *Keynes*. Glasgow: Fontana, 1976. A brief readable account of the life and work of the most influential economist of our age.

Robinson, Joan. *Contributions to Modern Economics*. New York, N.Y.: Academic Press, 1978. These essays by a foremost critic of conventional thinking provide both the substance and flavour of some of the debates among economists. Much of this selection is very accessible to the non-specialist.

About the Authors

GREGORY BAUM is professor of religious studies and sociology at the University of Toronto, and author of many books, including *Religion and Alienation, The Social Imperative, The Priority of Labour* and *Catholics and Canadian Socialism.*

DUNCAN CAMERON, professor of political economy at the University of Ottawa, is a frequent commentator on Radio-Canada and has contributed articles to the *Globe and Mail,* the *Financial Post, Canadian Forum* and *Policy Options.*

Also of Interest from James Lorimer & Company

Catholics and Canadian Socialism
Political Thought in the Thirties and Forties
GREGORY BAUM

Drawing on previously inaccessible material from the Depression era, Gregory Baum examines the hostility of the Catholic hierarchy to progressive social change—in particular the policies of the CCF—and three instances where new attitudes were advanced in spite of the church's official attitude.

"One of the best introductions available to the whole subject of the philosophical issues involved in socialism."
—*Books in Canada.*